WHEN LIGHTNING STRUCK THE OUTHOUSE

WHEN LIGHTNING STRUCK THE OUTHOUSE

A Tribute to a Great Coach
Ralph "Sporty" Carpenter

George Baker

PHOENIX INTERNATIONAL, INC.
FAYETTEVILLE

Inquiries should be addressed to:
Phoenix International, Inc.
17762 Summer Rain Road
Fayetteville, Arkansas 72701
Phone (479) 521-2204
www.phoenixbase.com

Frontispiece: Coach Carpenter dressed in his "full bulgalia," ready for practice.

Library of Congress Cataloging-in-Publication Data

Baker, George Golman.
  When lightning struck the outhouse : a tribute to a great coach Ralph "Sporty" Carpenter / George Golman Baker Jr.
       p. cm.
  Summary: "This book has been a labor of love that, in retrospect, came easy to me. I drew from sixteen years of daily contact with Coach Carpenter. I also garnered the thoughts of his friends, players, and opponents. We laughed long and hard almost every day. We passed along inside jokes that only he and I understood, most of which I cannot repeat in the interest of decorum. We traveled the world. We won and lost and suffered the outrageous slings and arrows of disgruntled fans. We tasted the sweet wine of victory and we left an indelible mark in the annals of small college football that is remarkable. He was, in the vernacular of my south Georgia upbringing, "much of a man!"" — Provided by publisher.
  ISBN 978-0-9835615-3-8 (pbk.)
  1. Carpenter, Ralph, d1990. 2. Football coaches—United States—Biography. 3. Henderson State University—Football—History. I. Title.
  GV939.C374B35 2012
  796.332092—dc23
  [B]

                                                                2011047111

Preface

Ralph "Sporty" Carpenter's Henderson State Reddies reached the eighth playing date of their 1981 schedule with a 7–0 record that rated them No. 1 in the NAIA.

They suffered an astonishing 27–16 upset at the hands of the Arkansas-Monticello Boll Weevils. They had been on a seven-year roll including four AIC championships and one trip to the national playoffs. The 1981 season that had packed so much early promise wound up 8–3.

Facing reporters after the UAM defeat, Sporty said, "Lightning struck the outhouse and we were in it." Or maybe that was how some cautious newspapers smoothed up some of his words in Sunday's sports sections the next day.

George Baker, one of Carpenter's longtime HSU assistants, has devoted a five-year labor of love to a biography of one of football's most captivating coaches.

Yes, "Lightning Struck the Outhouse" is part of the book title.

In a recent conversation, I asked George if he'd always planned to write about his favorite coach. He said no.

"Coach Carpenter died in 1990," he said. "Over the next few months, even the next few years, people would ask about the funny things he said and did, like jumping on the Southern Arkansas mule mascot after Henderson beat SAU. I guess that's what started me to thinking seriously about a book. And the deeper I got into it, the more fascinating it became.

"And the more I learned about him, I realized how kind and considerate he was, how many people he helped without ever saying anything about it. For example, I know he helped a lot of former players find jobs, either in coaching or something else. And especially how intelligent he was. He enjoyed being mistaken for a clown."

I met Sporty Carpenter in 1967 after he had joined the coaching staff of HSU, his alma mater, as an assistant to Clyde Berry. Sporty walked over to me, stuck out his hand, and said, "Hey, Scoop, Ralph Carpenter." Five or ten minutes later, he had everyone in the room laughing. He always used his formal name in introductions, although I don't recall anyone addressing him as Ralph.

He grew up in Hamburg ("The Burg," he usually called it), served in the navy, and played center and guard for Henderson before starting a succession of high school coaching jobs. Duke Wells, athletic director and former HSU coach, spotted potential in Carpenter. When a coaching vacancy occurred in 1970, Sporty was appointed head coach, obviously with Wells's approval.

"Sporty always liked for people to underestimate him," Wells said a few years later, when the Reddies were pretty much dismantling the AIC. "But he never fooled me."

Carpenter was head coach nineteen seasons, 1971–1989. His first two years were rebuilding chores. His teams went 119–76–5, .608, with five conference titles.

"I guess it turned out that all we needed was material," he said while HSU was going 10–1, 11–2, 11–1, 8–2, 9–2, etc.

In 1973, Sporty's Reddies broke through with an AIC championship, a 10–1 record and high ranking in the NAIA top 10. Their only loss, to Livingston State (now West Alabama), cost HSU a spot in the national playoffs.

Sporty was bitterly disappointed. His mood didn't improve when one of those small-college bowls (that used to pop up like toadstools) surfaced in an area of Georgia dominated by the chicken industry. This event was called the Poultry Bowl. The bowl sponsors extended an invitation to Henderson. The school declined to appear in what Sporty started calling "the Cluck Classic."

A newspaper reporter called Sporty and asked why his team was passing up the Poultry Bowl. "Just tell everybody we chickened out," he said.

As part of the buildup to the USA's 200th anniversary celebration in 1976, a Bicentennial Bowl was played in Little Rock's War Memorial Stadium in November 1975, with an 11–1 Henderson team impressively whipping an Oklahoma challenger.

Asked what he thought of the Bicentennial Bowl, Sporty turned diplomat. "I'm really looking forward to the next bicentennial game in 2175," he said.

From his earliest high school coaching jobs, Sporty would label a football player or team manager "Wedge" on the theory that "a wedge is about the simplest tool there is."

He claimed he once had an assistant coach who didn't mind being called Wedge, "but his wife sure didn't like being called Wedgenia."

If any football squad Sporty was associated with had an athlete named Waters, Sporty instantly dubbed him "Muddy." At least one of his "Muddy" guys was a big, strong fullback.

He came into Sporty's office after a game one day and said, "Coach, I played the whole game at fullback, but I only carried the ball twice. How could that be?" Sporty said, "Muddy, did it ever occur to you that it was designed that way?"

One day on a visit to the HSU campus, I walked into Sporty's office and found him preparing bulletin board material for his players. With tiny scissors, he would snip out any line of a newspaper article that didn't seem helpful in arousing the ire of his troops.

"You're wasting your time," I told Sporty. "Your kids will have seen all those stories in the papers, so cutting out some lines won't fool them."

Sporty laughed. "You don't know these guys, they don't read no newspapers."

By 1989, Sporty Carpenter was desperately ill, even to a layman's eye. He coached the team that fall, though. "It was the most courageous thing anyone could ever imagine," George Baker said.

"You know, Coach Carpenter always worked hard, daylight to dark, meetings, practices, but when the football staff was out eating dinner or something, Coach Carpenter would not allow anyone to mention football.

"Outside the office and the field, we weren't supposed to talk shop. Coach Carpenter thought twenty-three hours of football a day was enough."

—Jim Bailey
Longtime sportswriter for the *Arkansas Gazette* and later the *Arkansas-Democrat Gazette*

First Impressions

Often great friendships begin with small encounters. The first meeting I had with R. L. "Sporty" Carpenter occurred while I was working for his most intense rival, Ouachita Baptist University. Of course, in those days neither school was listed as a university, both were colleges. I had been hired by Buddy Benson as a graduate assistant in 1969 after I finished my tour of duty with the United States Army Infantry. The Vietnam conflict was going at a furious pace, and soldiers like me were escaping the possibility of returning to the conflict without much time to recover. I had returned from Korea, not Vietnam, but it was considered a combat tour as well. Coach Benson hired me as a full-time staff member in 1970 when Jimmy Jones decided to get out of football and take a job at his alma mater across the street. Being in the right place at the right time is better than being qualified and in the wrong place. I was highly unqualified at the time to do the job Coach Benson entrusted to me. I was defensive coordinator in the second year of my coaching career, not counting the two years I had coached in the army and the couple of years I had been a student assistant at Ouachita.

My duties at Ouachita included defensive coordinator, coaching the defensive line, dormitory supervisor, teaching fifteen hours, and generally running errands and doing any job that cropped up. I was happy to have the opportunity to coach on the college level, and I owe much to Coach Benson.

A few weeks after being released from the army, I found myself down on my knees scrubbing the toilets in the Ouachita field house, a large step down from being an officer and a gentleman. I was also finishing up the requirements for my master's degree by taking fifteen hours of graduate work.

At the time, Ouachita had a new piece of technology that Henderson had not acquired, the WATTS line. Coach Benson offered to let Coach Carpenter use the free telephone line as a favor. Coach Carpenter took him up on it, and the die was cast that would lead to my most significant professional relationship in my thirty-year coaching career.

One hot, muggy Arkansas summer night I got a call from Coach Benson asking me to open the gymnasium and his office for "Sporty" to use the WATTS line. I lived on campus and could be in front of the gymnasium in about fifty-nine seconds if I left then. I did. I got to the gymnasium before Coach Carpenter, and when he drove up and got out, I got my first close look at the man who was to become an important part of the rest of my life. I had seen him from across the field but had never met him.

I was young then, thirty years old and full of piss and vinegar, as Coach Carpenter would say. I took a close look at this man whom I had regarded as an enemy for the short time I had known his name. He had on his coaching garb, at that time khaki shorts, woolen athletic socks, Riddell big ripple coaching shoes, and an old HSTC tee shirt. Not too impressive a sight to a former officer who was used to seeing the big brass dressed up in their military finery.

"What do you say, Hoss?" He looked at me with a twinkle in his eye that seemed to say, "OK, we are not at the ready now; let's be friends." I had been involved with the Battle of the Ravine since they revived it in 1963 and was Ouachita through and through then. I have to admit I was guarded, dealing with the head coach of our archrival. The thought of ever working for this man never entered my mind.

We made some small talk, and I left him to the fairly long list of telephone numbers he brought on a clipboard. I gave him my phone number and asked him to call me when he finished so I could lock up. In a couple of hours he called and said, "I'm done, Hoss."

I jumped in my car and got over to the gymnasium just in time to see him drive off. One of my duties was to check the dormitory every night at 10:30, but this was summer, so I could just drive back to our little apartment to be with my lovely wife. Life was good!

I was called on several times that summer to "go let Sporty in." Each time we became a little more relaxed in our friendly banter. Coach Carpenter was a people person of immense depth. He had a country way of speaking and had a saying or epithet for almost every situation. He soaked up sayings like a camel at a water hole. In all the years that I knew him, I never knew him to fail to repeat a saying he heard earlier. It might be years, but sooner or later, I would hear it again. I am somewhat of a wordsmith and interested in vernacular, so I made it an unofficial study, listening and interpreting his sayings.

One thing I noticed right away—if you called him "Sporty," he was likely to hang a sobriquet on you. In the sixteen years I worked for Coach Carpenter, I never called him "Sporty." He rarely referred to me as anything but "George." Sometimes he would say Gorgeous, a play off "Georgiou's George," the iconic wrestler of the '50s and '60s, not my looks.

When Coach Carpenter took the head coaching reins from Clyde Berry in 1972, the program was in fine shape. Coach Berry is a fine man and an excellent coach. I got to know him after I crossed the Ravine in 1974. I also got to know the other fine men and women who were associated with Reddie athletics. I feel most fortunate to have been able to know and work with the truly great men and women on both sides of the Ravine.

Coach Duke Wells was the athletic director at Henderson in 1974 and I had known him since 1961. Coach Sawyer was assistant athletic director and track and cross-country coach. He was cut from the same fabric as Coach Wells, a fine, fine man who quietly went about his duties making his very busy schedule seem easy to casual observers. I really got to know and appreciate Coach Sawyer on the three-week European trip we took in 1976.

Not everyone you meet "gee haws" with you, as Coach Carpenter might say, but I found the athletic staff at Henderson to be so receptive to a Ouachita Tiger, fresh from the crossing of the mythical Ravine. Don Dyer, "Knocker," as Coach Carpenter and others of his era called him, was no exception. I never, in sixteen years, heard Coach Carpenter call Don anything but "Knocker." I will leave it to your imagination as to how Don acquired the moniker. Don and I became friends so easily; he is to Reddie basketball, what Coach Carpenter is to Reddie football. Both won at an unprecedented rate at HSU and both produced scholars, athletes, and good citizens. They both are unparalleled recruiters with the proverbial cauliflower ears from too many phone calls to prospects. Mentioning scholars in conjunction with football and basketball will probably provoke derisive exclamations from those who don't know the actual facts concerning athletics and academics. All the coaches with whom I have had the pleasure of working emphasized the importance of academics, without exception.

Consequently, athletes have a distinct advantage over non-athletes in that they have a staff of interested men or women seeing to their well-being athletically, socially, academically, and in some cases, spiritually.

These men and women I speak of here in the pages of this tribute were the "old school type of coaches." Sometimes, to their own detriment, they made decisions that hurt their record of winning or losing. I do not mean to say that winning was not important to them; I'm saying that they routinely made conscious choices that benefited individuals without regard to winning or losing.

I will pay them what I consider to be the highest compliment now by saying that I would be proud for any of them to coach my only son or my only daughter. Many of them are gone now, passed on, a part of the ages. Their names will live on as long as their players and the sons and daughters and grandsons and granddaughters and so on live to remember them.

Sometime during the football season of 1973, it became obvious to me that I needed to move on from Ouachita. Again, recalling the "better to be lucky than good" saying, a set of circumstances occurred that set into motion the events that would bring me to Henderson and a virtual career at one school.

As is common in families, Coach Benson and I were close; he was my hero while I played for him. Sometime during the five years I worked for him we developed a rift. I was headstrong and confident in my abilities and knowledge. He was a typically strong-willed, confident person, also. This caused clashes. I probably reacted inappropriately, and we came to "loggerheads." To make a long story short, one of us had to go, and it was obviously me. We parted.

I turned in my resignation early in the spring of 1974 and immediately started looking for a job. As is pretty well known, it is much easier to find a job if you have a job. I didn't know that then. Weeks went by and I didn't even have a nibble. One day while languishing in a men's clothing store in Arkadelphia, Don Wilkerson, who had been on the Reddie football staff for a couple of years, came in and announced that he had just resigned from his position at Henderson. I excused myself and went straight to my office in the Ouachita sports center and called Coach Wells and asked about the job.

Coach Wells verified that the position was open and had been for about thirty minutes. "How did you find out about this job so quickly?" he asked. I told him about my encounter with Don and he understood. He told me to send in my resume, and I would hear from them if I was chosen. I hung up with the feeling that my chances for that job were less than slim and none.

In the ensuing days and weeks I applied for several jobs, and again, no takers. I saw Don again a few weeks later, and he told me where he had applied. I just made a mental note of each place and went home and zipped a letter to all of them.

Lo and behold, I got an answer from Magnolia. Don Hubbard wanted me to come down and talk about being his offensive coordinator. He liked the East Texas Slot I we were running at Ouachita and asked if I could put it in for them. I allowed as to how I could, and he offered me the job. I was hesitant to take the offer as I had some irons in the fire that would potentially keep me at the college level. Don wanted an answer right now, and I understood his side of the situation. He called early one morning and told me his dad had had a heart attack and he had to go to visit him and he needed an answer right then. My son, who was a few months old then, had kept me up all that night with a high fever and I was a walking zombie, so I made a snap decision and said I would come. As soon as I hung up, I knew I shouldn't have taken the job.

A few nights later as I was working the national NAIA track meet on the Henderson campus, C. W. Keopple, head coach at Hall High School, asked me if I was interested in the defensive coordinator's job that had been created when his assistant coach Pat Jones departed for a graduate assistant job at the University of Arkansas. The Hall High job seemed better; it paid more and was in the largest class in the state, so I said I was interested. He offered me the job, and I called Don and made him angry, but it was in the best interest of my family.

C. W.'s wife was a real estate agent, so she started looking for a house for us. I went up to Hall and interviewed with all the proper people required for such a lofty position. All went well until C. W. told me that I was going to have to be Coach Oliver Elders' assistant basketball coach. I told C. W., whom I called coach also, that I didn't play basketball even in high school and that I didn't even watch it on TV. He said, "Well, the position calls for you to serve as assistant basketball coach. Go in there and talk to him." Coach Elders was an incredibly nice man, and he asked me what I knew about basketball. I told him the same thing I told C. W., and I could tell it didn't set well with him. They had a conference and C. W. came out and said, "He rejected you."

He then asked me to go back in Coach Elder's office and convince him that I knew a little about the sport. I went back in and told Coach Elders that I still didn't know anything about basketball, but that I had been around Bill Vining for a long time and that I would work very hard to help him. He looked troubled but grudgingly accepted me for his part of the job.

As we were looking for a house that day, I told Mrs. Keopple that I needed a house with a double carport. C. W. asked me why I needed a double carport because in those days most young families had only one car. I told him I had a bass boat. He said, "Oh, you won't need a bass boat."

I knew then that he planned for me to handle the weight program, discipline, study hall, etc., so he could inhabit the golf course every afternoon. I filed that bit of information in the back of my head and started thinking that I had made another poor decision.

A few nights later, my wife and I were playing cards with Bob Gravette and his wife when the phone rang, and when I answered it, Coach Carpenter was on the other end and he said, "Hoss, are you still interested in that job?" I took a deep breath and said, "Yes sir, I am."

He said in his inimitable way, "Sickle on over here in the morning and we will talk about it." The rest, as they say, is history—thirty-one years of history!

The next morning was a Saturday, a characteristically Arkansas

July day, hot and humid with out a breeze to stir the muggy air. I arrived at the Wells Building before eight o clock to find Coach's car already in the parking lot adjacent to the stadium.

I went into the coach's office to find Coach Carpenter sitting at his desk clipping articles from several local and statewide newspapers and jotting a note with each one and stuffing them into already-addressed envelopes. I learned later that this was a standard practice he had acquired as a part of his recruiting regimen. He had his pants legs rolled up and a waste-paper can between his knees and he was chewing Red Man chewing tobacco and spitting intermittingly into the can. The volume of expectorant already collected indicated that he had been there for quite some time!

I recall to this day the easy, relaxed manner with which Coach Carpenter went about introducing me to the various staff members who came in and out of the Wells Building that day. He had a way of putting one at ease and dealing with the matter at hand in such a way as to make one feel completely at home and in place. He never mentioned that I was hired or not, he just began filling me in on the football situation there at Henderson.

When lunch time came around there was no mention of breaking for a snack nor even getting a coke. Coach Carpenter was totally absorbed in football; he needed no other sustenance to maintain his high-octane pace. He literally existed on the adrenaline produced by his body in the excitement of the moment and the prospect of a coming season that promised to be a championship effort.

CHAPTER TWO

Becoming a Reddie

In the beginning with my job at Henderson, I had to learn a brand-new boss and the expectations of a new leader. Coach Carpenter was unlike any man for whom I had worked. He was somewhat like my father, an incredibly hard-working individual with the will to sacrifice himself for the task at hand. Coach Carpenter was determined to not allow opponents to out work him and his staff. He led by example, arriving at his office early and leaving late. I was used to long meetings and long days at Ouachita and in the military and also in working with my father. Coach Carpenter's days were longer, harder, and more regular! We worked eighteen hours a day, seven days a week most of the year. Immediately after hiring me Coach Carpenter called me and said, "George, sickle on over here Saturday morning and we will call some prospects." Well, I had been helping Billy Fred Jackson blow insulation for the past two summers and I had promised Billy Fred I would help him that particular Saturday. At the time of the promise I didn't have a job. I told Coach Carpenter about the commitment and that I felt constrained to keep my promise. His voice changed ever so slightly and he said, "OK, but I have a job and it is the only job I have." Nuff said! I knew the score and it was not hard to decipher. He expected me to be a full-time employee and from then on I was.

Coach Carpenter was a great guy for whom to work, he never asked me to do anything he would not do himself, and when it came to a dirty job, he was prone to do that chore himself.

I found him to be a man of unusual courage, allowing his assistants to coach without micromanaging them nor second guessing them. I loved his style of leadership and appreciated his leadership skills. In sixteen years he never once spoke to me in a disrespectful manner. I began to understand his method and became a fan of the man for whom I worked.

On my first day on the job he handed me a booklet with my name and defensive line coach typed on the front. Inside I found my job description and duties listed. Cut and dried, everything I needed to know about what I was to do in his system.

This was late July of 1974, the other coaches on the staff were Bradley Mills, a graduate of Kentucky who had played for the great Paul "Bear" Bryant, and Russell Cerrato, a Henderson graduate and veteran coach. Both of these men were as good as any coaches I ever encountered. I was to be defensive line coach for Bradley, who was the defensive coordinator. Russell was the offensive coordinator. We had two excellent graduate assistants, Darryl Horton and Larry Locke, and Coach Carpenter was the offensive line coach and head coach.

I soon learned that if I kept my mouth shut and listened to Bradley and Russell and Coach Carpenter I might learn some football. I did, and I did! The first year, 1974, we won eleven games and lost one, a pretty good start to my Henderson experience. We got into the NAIA Division 1 Playoffs and played in the finals against Texas A & I.

Texas A & I was at the top of the small college football food chain at that time and they were for real as we are prone to say these days. We had called around when we learned that A & I might be our opponent if we made it to the finals of the playoffs. I called East Texas State University in Commerce, Texas, because we knew most of the coaches on their staff and several of our professors had served as graduate assistants for the East Texas football staff while getting their graduate degrees—Lamar Watkins, Jimmy Jones, and a few others. I talked to the late Boley Crawford, who was known to be taciturn and a little gruff. I asked Boley if he thought we could beat

A & I. He said, "You cannot beat them." I informed him that we were a little small compared to A & I but we were "sudden," as Coach Carpenter might say. Boley said, "It don't make no difference 'cause you will fight through a 290-pound lineman to take on a 250-pound fullback that is blocking for a 225-pound tailback who holds national championship records in the one-hundred-meter dash!" Boley was too right and accurate in his description. He failed to mention that they were led on offense by a guy who was probably the best option quarterback in the country division one or two! He went on to be the quarterback coach for the University of Texas for several years after graduation from A & I.

I don't want to dwell too much on individual games but the finals of the NAIA championship was probably the zenith as far as games go for Henderson State University to this day. We won several conference championships later in my tenure at Henderson, returning to the playoffs again in 1985 where we lost to UCA in the semifinals after beating them soundly during the regular season. As Coach Carpenter put it, we lost our shooting taw in the first game of the playoffs and just didn't have the oomph to get over the hump with UCA in that second game.

At any rate, life on the Reddie football staff was much different than was life on the OBU staff. At Ouachita we met one night a week, played on Saturday, and met Sunday morning before breakfast and that was it. With Coach Carpenter the routine was like this: Meetings with your position coach before practice, practice, and break for supper and then meetings with your position coach after supper. After meeting with our players the coaches met again before finally dragging out of the Wells Building to perform dorm check at 10:00 p.m. That was Monday through Thursday. Friday night all coaches headed out to watch high school football games with the exception of one full-time coach who stayed home and met with the "troops." We rotated that duty unless one of the coaches had a son who played for Arkadelphia and in that case Coach Carpenter always saw to it that the individual with the son got the stay home duty on Friday nights when Arkadelphia played at home. He did not miss a detail in attempting to keep his coaches happy. I was able to see my son play most of his home games and some of his road games his last two years in high school, a gift for which I will be eternally grateful. Bradley Mills enjoyed the same privilege when his son Howard played for the Badgers. Not so little touches like this were just a few of the many thoughtful nuances in planning that marked the special vision of this good man.

When I approached him with a personal problem he was usually aware of the situation and was always willing to go the extra mile with me to help solve the dilemma.

After a few weeks on the job I realized that the man I was working for was more that the sum of his parts. I found him to be an exceedingly private man. His reputation of gregariousness belied his true demeanor. I was thirty-two years old and he was forty-two but his bearing and wisdom were unusual. The young men who were fortunate enough to play for him in those years got their full measure of the things they should have gotten. It is not original to speak of character, hard work, and the value of sacrifice for the good of all, loyalty, courage, confidence and scores of the things mankind knows to be essential in a person. R. L. "Sporty" Carpenter majored in those platitudes for the good of his men as well as for the good of the Reddie teams he tutored. He did not miss a thing! Being the head coach of the Reddies had long been a goal of his life. He reveled in the job and worked his heart out in making his dream a successful experience for his players and coaches.

I was fortunate enough to have a ride on the coat tails of one of the most visionary and erudite coaches to come along in the Arkansas Intercollegiate Conference since its inception. The old saying, I had rather be lucky than good, fits my happy circumstance to a tee! I was at the right place at the right time and good things happened for me. I settled in to this comfortable niche and began to enjoy the victories we racked up in 1974. We were 11 and 1 and loaded for bear for the season of 1975.

When we showed up for the annual chamber of commerce luncheon early in the fall of 1975, Coach Carpenter, in his characteristic generous manner, allowed each coach to briefly elaborate on his players. I was new man on the staff so I was last man to speak. After listing the talent I would be coaching I made a bold statement that astonished and literally angered some of the assistants and probably Coach Carpenter. I announced that if we lost a game this season they ought to fire us all! Coach Carpenter never mentioned the incident but I thought I was going to have to fight Bradley! He had been fired a few times already and I had been fired only once. Live and learn! I never made that mistake again.

We went 11 and 1 again in 1975. We lost to Ouachita the last game of the season. We were an excellent team. We pitched five shutouts that season. Our offense was not the best but managed to score enough points to win eleven games. Ouachita was also an excellent team with Billy Vining quarterbacking the East Texas I type of offense that Jimmy Jones, a Henderson graduate, had put in for Coach Benson in the season of 1969. Benson had tweaked the offense and made it his own over the previous seven years. It was a stunning array of sweeps, draws, screens, and reverses combined with the pinpoint accuracy of Billy Vining's pro type arm. The combination of those things was enough to cause defensive coordinators to pull out their hair and lose sleep the week before they played the Tigers. I was coaching the defensive line and I will not mention the state-of-the-art holding that Tommy Murphree, OBU's offensive coordinator, had taught his offensive line! I don't want to take anything away from their victory but they would grab my defensive linemen and fall over backward pulling my pure-hearted young men down with them. It was very hard to catch and they got few holding calls until the officials caught on, which was years later!

I never doubted for a moment that we would be victorious. I was supremely confident! The game started as I expected, we scored and kicked the extra point, 7 to zip. We played some more and scored again, we missed the extra point and it was 13 to zip. The small voice deep inside my conscious mumbled something about missed points coming back to haunt you but the fact that we had given up only a handful of points that year pushed that pesky little critter right back where he belonged. Then they scored! It was 13 to 7 after they made their extra point. We battled some more and scored again. OK, we made the extra point and it became 20 to 7, a virtual runaway with our defense!

Then the unbelievable occurred, they scored again! They kicked the extra point and it was a ball game again, 20 to 14. Manageable but scary, now the little voice was screaming, "I told you so!" I pushed it away again voicing confidence in our defense. Late in the fourth quarter Billy Vining quarterbacking a smaller but skillful offense ran into that defense and with just a couple of minutes left in the game he dropped back and hit our drop end square in the numbers. Ricky Minter from Nash, Texas, who has gone on to coach at Notre Dame, Kentucky, North Carolina, and to be the head coach at Cincinnati, intercepted the ball and was tackled immediately. As he trotted off the field with about a minute and 50 seconds left on the clock, I patted him on the fanny as coaches are prone to do and declared, "Way to go, boy, you just won the game."

Ouachita with its powerful offense ran three plays and the score-board stats revealed that the down was fourth and the distance was twenty-five! There were about twenty seconds left on the clock so OBU had no choice but to go for it. At this point I witnessed a set of circumstances occur that reinforces the idiom, it ain't over till its over!

After Minter's interception we were on the plus end of the field with the ball and less than two minutes to go in the game. We were in the virtual catbird seat, so to speak. The fat lady had not sung yet but I could hear her warming up behind the bleachers! On the first play from scrimmage after intercepting Vining's pass, our freshman tailback coughed up the ball and the Tigers pounced on it.

Our great defense would have to win the game for us. No problem, I told the little voice.

To the uninformed, there is no game plan for a fourth and twenty-five situation. Maybe a Hail Mary or what ever Baptists do but it is just not a tenable situation. A couple of weeks before Ouachita had run a hide-out play against Mississippi College and we had covered it with our defense. On this particular situation, Ouachita was in a panic and we were darn near the same. We were screaming "watch the draw, watch the pass, watch whatever" and they huddled with twelve guys. That was before the rule that forbids multiple numbers in the huddle and requires only eleven men in the huddle had been passed. The twelfth man broke the huddle and realized he was an extra slot back so he sprinted for the sideline. Our All American cornerback saw him exit and followed him over to the sideline as he called our double cover man off their tight end, who happened to be their best receiver! "Hide out, hide out!" he screamed, and Bradley Mills screamed, "Timeout, timeout!" but it was too late. Billy Vining had seen the whole thing and had audibled to a route for their uncovered receiver and he caught the pass for twenty-five yards and one inch. Our safety, Wilbert Hunter knocked the guy out but he held on to the ball, a couple of plays later with just seconds left on the clock Ken Stuckey caught a curl route from Billy Vining for the TD and when their try for point was good we were knocked out of an undefeated season by our rivals from across the ravine. "Divine providence," they cried. "Fickle fate," we responded, but I am here to tell you, it wasn't funny one bit!

A couple of weeks later Ouachita made their first-ever appearance in the NAIA playoffs and were soundly defeated by Salem, West Virginia. OBU's field was in terrible shape from a game they had played in the rain against UA PB a few weeks earlier so OBU had to play the game on our field, adding the proverbial insult to the terrible injury.

As luck would have it, we had the opportunity to play in a post-season game at War Memorial Stadium that year. We played East Central Oklahoma, coached by Pat O'Neal. East Central was well respected and one of the best teams in the country that year and we whipped them pretty good, 28 to 14. The combination of our victory and OBU's defeat put us ahead of them in the final NAIA poll, a fact that gave us little solace. Later on we were to learn that the NAIA was sponsoring a European trip designed to increase the popularity of American football on the Continent. At that time no American college teams had ever played in Europe. When we first heard the rumor it was to be four teams but in the end it became only two. Henderson State and at that time Texas A & I, now known as Texas A & M at Kingsville, got to make the trip of a lifetime. We spent three weeks playing each other in some of the most desirable cities in Europe. We played in Berlin, Nuremburg, and Manheim, Germany, and in Vienna, Austria, and Paris, France. We played five games and the Reddies won all but five of the games.

Circumstances surrounding our being chosen for the trip of a lifetime includes the astute and visionary way Coach Carpenter approached the NAIA hierarchy. As soon as he became the head coach at Henderson State he began a campaign to make the Reddies well known nationally. Heretofore there was an almost opposite mindset. The old Arkansas Intercollegiate Conference (AIC) was basically a low-budget, low-profile group of almost clannish education-minded institutions with an ambivalent repute nationally. Ouachita had made some national ripples with basketball in the sixties and Arkansas Tech played in the football finals in 1971 but other than that, the standing of the conference nationally was pretty much a well-kept secret.

The AIC football teams regularly played nearby teams from the surrounding states and fared well with the lower-level teams in their class. We loved to play the Oklahoma directional schools, North West, South East, South West, and East Central to name a few. We did not like the Louisiana schools because they had a size and program/scholarship advantage.

Coach Carpenter, by the time he became head coach at HSU, was well aware of the effect scheduling had on your record and that win-loss records were the only thing people remembered after the game was over. He immediately began to schedule some "Chitins," as he called them, to bolster his nonconference docket.

He worked untiringly, spending countless hours on the phone communicating with the prominent programs in the NAIA and picking and choosing parts of the ones he thought to have an astute coach or athletic director. The European trip was, in my opinion, a direct result of this extra work. I have never heard anyone else mention this fact. The old saying, when you find a turtle on a fence post, he didn't get there by himself, did not apply here. The public, in general, has a tendency to see things happen and hang the cause on a nail of choice, either, gosh what happened or how did that happen or what happened. In the case of the European trip very few people even knew it happened. We got more press in Europe than we got in Arkansas!

We were the first American colleges to play American football in Europe, for gosh's sake! It is a fact that cannot be duplicated. It's done, we did it, and the man to whom the credit is due as far as getting the Reddies to Europe, got little acclaim for the accomplishment.

Coach Carpenter with his game face on. Note the Red Man bulge in his cheek.

Three rugged Reddies pose on Old Haygood Field, circa 1956. *From left,* Sporty Carpenter, Dwight Adams, and John Greenwood, two of Coach Carpenter's best friends. *Courtesy of John Greenwood.*

Sporty and Sabra in 1956 at John Greenwood's home in Arkadelphia, a handsome couple indeed!

Sporty and Sabra with Bobbie Johnson at the airport in Berlin on the European tour of 1976.

Coach George Baker, Coach Carpenter, and a couple of the cheerleaders who accompanied the Reddies on the European tour of 1976.

George Baker, Sporty Carpenter, and Brother Bob Trieschmann in front of the Eiffel Tower in Paris, France, 1976. How are you gonna keep them down on the farm?

Brother Bob Trieschmann, George Baker, and Coach Sporty Carpenter taking a much-needed break from sightseeing in Paris, 1976.

The Raphael portrait of Count Baldassare Castiglione seems to be gazing at something across the room and Coach Carpenter, Billy Bock, and Brother Bob Trieschmann all have turned to see what it is, in the Paris Louvre, 1976, European tour.

Coach George Baker surveying the mountain of equipment taken on the European tour. We learned too late that we had to personally transport all that gear! *Courtesy of Carl Humphries.*

Coach Jim Mack Sawyer, who acted as our athletics director on the tour, negotiates with an official in a restaurant as George Baker looks on with a "Cheshire cat" smile. Coach Bradley Mills is in the background. *Courtesy of Carl Humphries.*

Coach George Baker is standing, while Coach Carpenter, Coach Mike Deal, and Coach Billy Bock take a load off their feet at the Olympic Stadium in Berlin. *Courtesy of Carl Humphries.*

Carl Humphries strolling away from one of the most iconic landmarks in the world, European tour, 1976. *Courtesy of Carl Humphries.*

Carl Humphries, student manager, enjoys the dizzying heights of the Eiffel Tower, European tour, 1976. *Courtesy of Carl Humphries.*

Coach Jim Mack Sawyer, Coach Sporty Carpenter, and Coach Billy Bock in front of our hotel in Nuremburg, Germany. The restaurant next door would not serve us water with our meals, wishing to sell us beer. We had our players find a grocery store and buy water or soft drinks to have with our meals. *Courtesy of Carl Humphries.*

Bradley Mills, Billy Bock, and George Baker plot their next move in the Paris Louvre. *Courtesy of Carl Humphries.*

Coach Sporty Carpenter enjoys a cigar atop the Eiffel Tower, European tour, 1976.
Courtesy of Carl Humphries.

Coach Sporty Carpenter "glad hands" an American general in Nuremburg, Germany. The military greeted us with open arms and fed us on the base there in Nuremburg one night for a welcome taste of good old American food. *Courtesy of Carl Humphries.*

Coach Sporty Carpenter puffs on his stogie as Coach George Baker cools his tired dogs in Nuremburg, Germany, 1976. *Courtesy of Carl Humphries.*

A line-up of the complete coaching staff during the time of the European tour. *From the top on the left side in descending order:* Coach John Duke Wells, Coach Betty Wallace, Coach Bradley Mills, Coach Sporty Carpenter, and Coach George Baker. *From the top on the right side:* Coach Jim Mack Sawyer, Coach Jane Sevier, Coach Dee Brumfield White, Coach Bobby Reese, Coach Don Dyer, and Coach Billy Bock.

Coach George Baker on the game field for one of our Friday practices. *Courtesy of Randy Clift.*

From left, Paul Calley, Gus Malzahn, Dexter Lewis, and Coach Sporty Carpenter doing PR work in a local bank.

Coach John Duke Wells and Coach Sporty Carpenter in front of the Wells building making a press release photo, circa 1976.

Nine players from Florida, all contributors and all recruited by Reddie alumni: *Front row from left to right:* Terry "Pump" Calkins, Paul Robinson, Joe Smith, "Bubba" Smith (no relation to Joe). *Back row from left to right:* John "Kitch" Kitchens, Stan "Ears" Riner, Virgil Green, Joey Green (brothers), and Eddie Fullwood.

Keith "Bozo" Bryan kicking a field goal in the 1985 semifinal game vs. Central Oklahoma. Central was ranked number one in the nation that day.

Gus Malzahn, Paul Calley, Dexter Lewis, and Coach Carpenter do PR work at a local bank.

Keith "Bozo" Bryan kicks the game-winning field goal in the NAIA semifinal game vs. number one in the nation Central Oklahoma, 1985.

Coach Billy Bock giving Robert Hester one of his patented pep talks during a timeout.

Robert Hester kicks off for the Reddies, circa 1976-77.

Paul Calley, center, Wayne Davenport, student manager, and Gus Malzahn, defensive back and punter, visit a local bank to garner support for the Reddie football team.

Jeff Atkinson, linebacker, circa 1986.

Charley Boyd, poster boy for tenaciousness. Charley was one of a long list of overachievers who were nurtured by Coach Carpenter.

Photo arranged by Chris "Big Earl" Campbell.

#28 CHARLIE BOYD

1975 ~ 1978 Henderson State University
1975 ~ 11-1, 1976 ~ 8-2, 1977 ~ 9-2, 1978 ~ 7-2-1
Overall Record 35-7-1

1975 Bicentennial Bowl
Little Rock, Ar.
HSU 27 ~ EC Oklahoma 14

1976 European Tour Played
Texas A&I in 6 exhibition games
on a 21 day tour of Europe

1975 AIC Champs   1976 AIC Runner-up
1977 AIC Champs   1978 AIC Runner-up

A good time to be a Reddie.

Coach Carpenter gives Jim Ford the play during a game in 1974.

Dean "Deano" Norsworthy, one of the many young men who benefited from his experience with Coach Carpenter and the Reddie football program.

1970 Reddie baseball team, AIC Champions. Mr. Harry "Mr. B" Butler is to the far left, Mr. B always had his "want to" ready! Coach Carpenter is to the far right.

1963 Wynne Yellow Jacket team photo. The coach on the far left is Spriggs Nutt, who was the basketball coach and assistant to Sporty in football. Coach Carpenter is to the far right.

Wynne Yellow Jackets, 1963, with Cliff Garrison. Sporty was head coach and Cliff was one of his assistants. Both went on to be highly regarded in their respective sports. Cliff in basketball and Sporty in football.

Ralph "Sporty" Carpenter with his friend and fellow coach, Ronnie Bailey, at Liberty Eylau High School, where they led the team to the finals of the state championship.

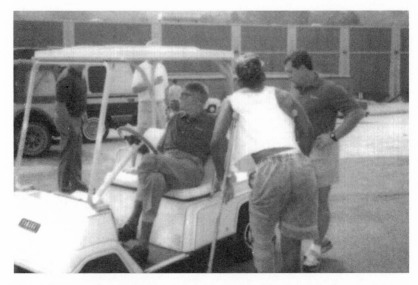

Coach Carpenter in golf cart his last year to coach the Reddies, 1989. Perry Godell is to the far right; Wayne Davenport is the young man on crutches.

Coach Sporty Carpenter with his usual positive demeanor.

Sayings

Coach Carpenter had a million sayings; he literally exuded folksy anecdotes and ribald southern humor epithets. I will attempt to list and explain as many of these as I can remember and I hope to be reminded of others as the stories I am collecting come in to my project. These will be in no particular order, just random recollection as I journey through the sixteen years we walked the same paths.

The boards are hard and the nails are rusty! Sometimes called out in practice when the spirit of the moment overcame him and he just had to exclaim something. The players seldom knew what the words meant but understood the mood. This is probably one of his top sayings.

Bang went the egg money! Uttered over the field phones when an opponent broke a long run or captured the momentum from the offense. Coach Carpenter never became rattled on the sidelines; he kept a cool head and never harassed his assistants. He watched his area of personal coaching, for example, the offensive line, and allowed no one but himself to correct or adjust his beloved "DOGS."

Let's gin! His way of letting the offensive coordinator know he wanted to run the ball. This is about as strong a hint as he ever used to make known his opinion on the play selection. He was a proponent of letting his coaches coach. This is one of his most-endearing characteristics, in my opinion. He made one feel empowered and he expected one to take ownership in the program.

Run the goose. He would run plays in from the sideline, and this is the term he used to call the quarterback sneak. It sometimes caused confusion early in the year when we did not call it the goose in practice because I called all plays in practice in person and he repeated the plays from my calls from the press box. I would say, "01 or 02, consistent with our offensive numbering system," and he would tell the runner, "run the goose." When the runner arrived in the huddle and called "the goose," many times the QB would say, "What?" and the result might be a delay of game penalty. We ironed that out quickly and remained on the same page most of the time.

Goat hair. Any player with tight curly hair. There were several during my tenure. I never remember a player objecting to a nickname given him by Coach Carpenter. They knew the spirit in which the names were imparted.

Hog Jowls. A name reserved for larger players with full faces.

Nickel Nose. He used this expression to describe someone whose nostrils were prominent.

Bubble Butt. A self-explanatory label.

Red on the Head. Red-haired person.

Red ace Green. Also a red-haired person.

Grease your gums. Eat.

Raw Butt. Anyone named Robert.

Cam Dam. Camden.

El dora doo. Eldorado.

MEMORIES

Alan Nance
>Friend and fellow student at HSU

Well, the first thing is that Sporty just had a way with boys; he knew how to get the best out of them. Sporty had everyone at heart. He had a nickname for everyone. He was always upbeat and a lot of fun to be around. I just loved to be around him. I could get around him and Ronnie Bailey and I would laugh all day.

I first met him at Henderson. Did anyone tell you 'bout the Arkansas Tech cheerleader story? It was down at the tavern across from the campus. It was game day for a basketball game, Sporty was a manager on the team, and we were in the tavern when in walks a couple of Tech's cheerleaders. One of them was a tall skinny kid and he had a little "pork pie hat" on his head. Sporty looked him over and said, "Hey, scat daddy, give me that hat." Of course the young man refused and allowed as to how he needed the hat. Sporty was determined to get the hat and things began to go south and they decided to take it outside and settle it in an honorable fashion true to the established redneck rules of engagement. When they squared off, only two licks were passed, the cheerleader hit Sporty and Sporty hit the ground. It seems that Sporty had had the misfortune of challenging a golden gloves boxer who was intramural boxing champ on the Tech campus. Sporty wore dark shades for about a week to hide the shiner the cheerleader had given him.

I knew that Sporty attended The University of Arkansas at Monticello, I had a friend down there named O. L. "Flash" Pierson. O. L. told me a story on Sporty that concerned a Gene Krupa concert that was coming to the campus and Sporty kind of idolized Krupa and wanted to go to the concert, but didn't have a white shirt.

O. L. said that he had one white shirt to his name, but agreed to loan it to Sporty for the concert so he could attend. According to O. L. the next morning he awoke to see Sporty lying on the floor in their dorm room with O. L.'s only white shirt covered with a large autograph in lipstick of "Gene Krupa" across the front!

He was here and the Lord put him here for a good purpose. He knew how to use the God-given talent he had. Everybody loved him. He knew how to talk to people and get the best out of them. He had a caring heart.

Alvin Futrell

Former student and athlete at Wynne High School and later colleague at Henderson State University

The man "Coach Sporty Carpenter" was a unique individual who loved people and loved helping people, especially young people. I had the privilege of meeting Coach Carpenter during my senior year at Wynne High School. We had just completed the basketball season and I was going to finish the remainder of the year in study hall, since I had all the credits needed to graduate. As I sat in study hall, in came Coach Carpenter, who said to me, "Hoss, come with me." Then he proceeded to tell me, "Hoss, you will be competing in track and not wasting your time in study hall." That was the beginning of a long relationship.

Coach Carpenter was also very instrumental in my attending Henderson State. I remember him carrying me to the state basketball tournament at Barton Coliseum in Little Rock and introduced me to Coach Don Dyer, the head basketball coach at Henderson State. The irony here is when I entered Henderson in the fall as a freshmen, Coach Carpenter also joined the Henderson football coaching staff and was very supportive of me throughout my college career.

After four years of military service and a year of graduate school,

I was fortunate enough to join the Henderson faculty. Sporty Carpenter became more to me than just a coach. He became my colleague, friend, advisor, mentor, and confidant. At this point I had the opportunity to see Coach Carpenter, the total package. I witnessed him providing young boys opportunities to go to college, to play football, and to get an education when other coaches and schools would not. I watched him guide, mold, and discipline these young boys as they developed into young men. He was their parent away from home. But what's more important, Coach Carpenter possessed a genuine love for his players. Not only did he insist that they graduate, he also assisted them in becoming gainfully employed and maintained close communication with them after they left Henderson.

Sporty Carpenter not only touched the lives of his players, students, colleagues, and friends, but he made a difference in the lives of those who came in contact with him. Sporty is a legend that lives on in all of us who knew him.

Andy O'Mara
    Football letterman, Henderson State University

Coach Baker, I'm sorry to be so slow to get back to you but I can only come up with one small personal anecdote about Coach Carpenter. It happened during spring practice, probably in 1984.

I was not having a very productive spring. I'd been sluggish and wasn't working very hard. I don't remember why, I just wasn't having a very good spring. One day in practice we were working on the goal line against the defense and not doing very well. After one play, I don't know if I missed a block or went the wrong way but, when I got back to the huddle he was waiting on me. I knew he was behind me and all he did was say something, kind of low, not very loud. Something like "Omar, you ain't working very hard, you need to get your butt in gear." Of course, the next play I got the ball and ran over a couple guys and scored from about six yards out. That was all I needed for the rest of the spring. I guess he knew I needed a little push to get going. He was like that.

I always appreciated him giving me a chance to play. I first came to HSU in the spring of '82. I had visited the previous fall during homecoming but hadn't talked to him since. The day before we were supposed to report he called me at home in Springdale and asked if I was gonna come down. I told him I didn't have the money. I think he talked to my dad for about five minutes. When he hung up my dad told me to pack my bags, he would loan me the money for school. Still don't know what he said but I doubt I would have my degree without his help.

Bayan Abraham
  Football letterman, Henderson State University

Coach Baker,

I think it is wonderful that you're writing a book. Especially about a man that touched many people's lives. "Sporty" Carpenter was as good a man as they come, coach, teacher, friend, and to me, FAMILY. Sporty was a man of few words that made a lot of impact on people, he got his point across real fast. His famous one-liners will be with me forever "YOU'RE AS USELESS AS TITS ON A BOAR"; "THIS AIN'T NO BARNYARD"; "YOU'RE BURN-ING DAYLIGHT"; and "THIS AIN'T NO REST CAMP, SON." Wow, he was so comical and in the same sentence so serious. He helped people in need in a quiet manner. He was known and respected by everyone in our league and around Arkansas.

As far as I go when it came to Sporty, he was my father figure away from home. He always made sure I was OK with everything and had a place to go on holidays and what not. He made sure I stayed out of trouble and hit the books. He's had personal chats with my professors making sure I did what I was supposed to. Sporty and I have had numerous one-on-one talks about life, and what I was going to do after football. Seems like everything turned out OK for me and my family. I give a lot of thanks to Sporty—for that may he rest in peace and God have mercy on his soul.

Bill Cook

My first year at Henderson was 1971, as you will recall, the weight room used to be in the old Arkadelphia Country Club House. The team had started growing mustaches in the off season as was the style of the time. Of course, Sporty said at that time no, there's no way we are going to have mustaches. I remember that he got every body out of the weight room and we sat out there under the shade trees and he just talked to everybody. Of course, some of the players said we want them; it's in style now and all that kind of stuff. There was a lot of discussion with the assistant coaches and all that kind of stuff. I remember staying after the meeting broke up, along with several of us, and talking to Coach Carpenter and convincing him that the mustaches weren't going to have any influence on how a kid played football. It was a rough decision for a young coach to make because at that time, the University of Arkansas and most programs didn't allow long hair or facial hair. I remember after that meeting, after a few days Sporty was convinced that he had made the right decision. He didn't want it to cost him players and, of course, history has proven him right. The times were changing and Sporty recognized that he needed to make that change. I really admired him for being able to make that change.

Sporty was just like a dad to me and so many other young men who came under his influence. You could talk to him and he would listen.

I had him in an officiating class, so he had me as the ball boy during football games. I would run out there and swap balls during a timeout or a penalty. I would listen to what the official said and then sprint back to the sidelines and tell Sporty what they were saying so he could make the decision.

We were playing Samford University in the season of 1972, it was Duke Wells Day, we had a huge crowd. The ROTC color guard was there and this was supposed to be Samford's last year to play football. On the first play of the game, Samford lined their team up on the sidelines, their complete team all had their toes on the sideline, and they ran the hide-out play, tossed a little pass and scored on us, no one was even around the receiver. Neither Sporty nor any of his assistants saw what happened; they just thought the defensive back messed up. Well, we got the ball, ran three or four plays and punted it back to them, and they ran three or four plays and ran the hide-out play again and scored again. So, Sporty is chewing on the defensive back again. So he said, "Cook, run over on the other side and see what's going on over there." So I ran around the track to the other sideline and I'm standing there and they do it again. Well, Billy Miller, who was our punter and the defensive back on that side, didn't see the guy again because he was obscured by the Samford players standing on the sideline. So I yelled, "Hey, Billy, here's your man over here," and Billy came over and covered him and the scheme was busted. About that time, the Samford offensive line coach grabbed me by the neck and threw me out into the track and said, "Get your little ass back over on your sideline where you belong!" I went back to the Reddie sideline and Sporty asked, "What's happening over there, boy?" I told him the Samford coach had told me to get back to where I belong and Sporty laughed and said, "Are you going to let him scare you off, boy?"

Author's note: When Coach Carpenter recounted this story as he did many times, he said that the following Sunday when the team watched the film, it became obvious what was happening, and it also revealed Bill Cook and David Carpenter, who was a small boy, sprinting around the track after being tossed by the opposing coach.

C. D. Taylor
Boys' State friend

We were at Boys' State one year and back then, long hair wasn't very popular with the staff. Sporty and I shared the same barracks and we had this old boy from Jasper, Arkansas, who had hair down to his shoulders. Sporty told me, "You need to get him a haircut." I said, "Why don't you cut it?" He said, "We'll get him." So, whenever we got together in a group Sporty would announce, "The barber is going to be here tomorrow night." That old boy wouldn't let on, like that didn't affect him. So anyway, every time Sporty would see that old boy he would say, "The barber's going to be here tomorrow night."

Well, I guess he said it one time too many, 'cause Sporty yelled to the boy that afternoon, "Hey, Jasper, the barber's coming tonight." The old boy said, "That SOB ain't cutting my hair," and he packed up that night and left Boys' State.

Charles Dunn
President at Henderson for many years

Remembering Ralph "Sporty" Carpenter

Sporty was one of the first people I met when I first came to Henderson as its 14th president in February, 1986. I recall that we went to a basketball game at the Wells Center and the family was introduced at halftime. We were standing in the middle of the basketball court and, suddenly, about 75 or 80 of the biggest guys I'd ever seen came storming out of the stands and surrounded us. They, along with Sporty, presented us with "Reddie" shirts from the Henderson football team. That was how I first met Sporty Carpenter.

Soon after that he came by my office to take me down to Haygood field so I could see the football facilities. He was driving his old red truck, of course. As we walked out on to the field . . . in that marvelous stadium built into a bowl . . . he said "Doc, if I can get a recruit to walk down here on this field, I've got 'em." He was a great recruiter . . . spent terrific numbers of hours on the phone . . . so it was not unusual for 100–125 players to show up in the fall. I asked him why he needed so many. He said "Uniforms are pretty cheap. Lots of these kids won't get to play, but they are part of the team anyway." I thought that was a pretty good strategy for recruiting kids to Henderson and giving them a ready-made place to find friends and connections. It worked.

Unfortunately, Sporty was not in very good health by the time I got here. That caused him to react to criticisms that, in the past, he would have ignored completely. I recall that he received an anonymous letter criticizing his record as coach. He brought it to me along with an envelope that I concluded was a letter of resignation. When he told me his intentions, I told him that I hated to see him driven off by a letter that wasn't even signed. "Do what I did," I told him. "Throw it in the trash." I told him to hold on to his letter and talk with me tomorrow if he still wanted to resign. The next day, he and Jim Mack Sawyer came to the office. Sporty said "Did you mean what you said when you said you wanted me to stay on as coach?" I replied that I did . . . that few others cared for the students like he did. In a show of emotion, he hugged me and said "You know I've learned something today. You aren't just our preppy president . . . you've got heart." I am prouder of that comment that most other compliments I've received in my career. Sporty definitely had heart!

Charlie Boyd

Player, Coach Carpenter's lawyer, friend

PREFACE

I was at Henderson State from 1975 through 1979, and George Baker was one of my coaches this entire period of time. He bestowed upon me the privilege of contributing to this book, and, within the time allotted, the limitations of my writing skills, and the memory problems associated with the passage of time, I have attempted to fulfill this task. However, the biggest problem associated with my contribution is the enormity of the task at hand. How do you sit down with a pen and a piece of paper and write a chapter on Coach Carpenter? More importantly, how does a fifty-four-year-old man put into writing how someone affected him during a four-year period of time in his life that transpired over thirty years ago? Better yet, how do you codify how that someone is a part of who you are today, and your interactions with people every day, when this occurs subconsciously and/or you don't know how you're going to react to something that occurs ten minutes from now because that hasn't happened yet? The answer is simple: You can't. Where do you begin, and where do you end? As the lyrics from the old Eagles' song say: "What to leave in, and what to leave out." It is impossible for me to begin, and end, my memory of Coach Carpenter, along with those teammates from ol' Goodloe Dorm, in any way that could be termed "succinct."

No coach, teammate, cheerleader, band member, teacher, or fellow student at HSU that I have not mentioned by name has been forgotten. This book is about Coach Carpenter, and make no mistake, he is the "Leader of the Band." But all of us who are members of the "Reddie Family" and knew him were touched by him, not only uniquely and individually, but also cumulatively. If at any point in this chapter I am speaking of me (or my family, my friends, and especially my father), or my life, it is also about Coach Carpenter. Because the two cannot be totally separated, and sometimes the best way to write about someone who is a part of you, is to offer oneself up as a perspective. And once the genie squirms out up to her waist, you can't put her back in the bottle. Memories lead to more memories. People and places. Events and faces. At some point you just have to stop, lest you feel like the "Thinking Man." Sitting naked on a rock; trapped for eternity with your chin in your hand, trying to sort out things that don't bother Bubba and Elrod at all. Too much for both of us to ever figure out, and, unlike him, I'm trapped by a single lifetime, and mortality.

Finally, I am not William Shakespeare, William Faulkner, nor Mark Twain, and there is a "sliding scale" difference between a symphony, classical music, and a rock and roll band. While I cannot divorce myself from over three decades of being a lawyer, I am much more comfortable around, and fond of, those individuals with whom I share a common bond; a "melting pot" of young men who came to love a school and, more so, a coach. This chapter is composed of language that is a hybrid cross between the prose of legalese, and the jargon and slang of a Chicot County farm boy who came to *deeply* love a coach. If you want to read *Macbeth, The Sound and the Fury,* or *The Adventures of Tom Sawyer,* do so. My contribution is for "us."

Therefore, with that predicate, and based on a memory which may differ from others, I reduce to writing my contribution. Some people say that writing a chapter in a book like this is a sad event because you "turn loose" of an individual. I do not believe I will ever turn loose of Coach Carpenter, and hope that somehow I can portray to the reader the basis for that statement with the following.

I
THE MOMENT

I will never forget the day. Midafternoon on February 16, 1990. I was sitting in my office at the Davidson Law Firm, grinding it out. It's about that time of the day when you get a little groggy, whatever exuberance your assistants had for your occupation (and your company) normally begins to ebb, and at that age I became onerously oppressive, riding them to keep "pushing it" and to get whatever's on the plate done.

I had not heard from Coach Carpenter in a long time, and, as all of you know, his voice is unmistakable.

> Chally.
> Hey, Coach, what's going on?
> I'm flat on my back and I ain't gonna make it.
>> (Long Pause)
>
> ————————
>
> What do you mean, Coach?
> They gettin' ready to wheel me in to the operating room for a liver transplant, and I ain't gonna make it.
>> (Long Pause)
>
> ————————
>
> Oh, you gonna make it, Coach.
> No, Chally, I'm flat on my back and I ain't gonna make it. I need you to do something for me.
> Sure, Coach, anything you want, but you *are* gonna make it. You are.
> Now listen to me, Chally, this is what I want you to do, and I'm asking you because I know you'll get it done for me. I want you to prepare my *Last Will and Testament,* and leave my body to medical research in honor of all the boys who have worn the Red and Gray for me through the years, in memory of how happy and joyful they've made my life, so that somebody else will benefit. You put the right words in it, and make it legal. But that's what I want you to do.

When do you need it?

Right now. I don't know how much time I've got.

When is your surgery scheduled?

I'm waitin' in line.

Coach, it's an hour and a half drive to Memphis. I'll
be there in two and a half hours.

I was stunned. Stunned to the point that I was paralyzed. It is one of those moments in life when time stands still, the world stops turning, and you are consumed by the moment. After a long pause, I realized that if I was going to keep my word to Coach Carpenter, I had better pick up a dictaphone.

I do not have a copy of the document I prepared, having moved my office since I prepared same, and it has been misplaced. However, if I may paraphrase, the operative language read as follows:

> I *Will* my heart, body, and soul to medical science, in
> honor of all the young men who have worn the Red and
> Gray for me through the years, in recognition of the joy
> and happiness they have brought to me, and how they
> have fulfilled my life, and gave part of their heart, body,
> and soul to me, so that others might benefit and *live*.

This was Coach Carpenter's idea and wish; it is not hyperbole made up by me. In a nutshell, it speaks far greater than any treatise from me as to how he felt about his players, and what he had done with his life. His players were his life. I remember when his son, Sporty Jr., received the High School Coach of the Year Award and, during his acceptance speech, made a comment as a basis for some action he had taken to the effect: "That's what I'm doing because that's what's best for the boys, and that's what the boys want." He sounded just like a chip off the old block.

Some of my memories from that telephone call, and that day, are vivid, and with some I have difficulty. To make an analogy, eyewitnesses to the John F. Kennedy assassination were interrogated, and recorded statements obtained, immediately after President Kennedy was shot. Thirty years later, those exact same witnesses were interviewed with regard to the events that transpired, and what they had witnessed. It was amazing to the investigators how their stories had changed over the years as to pertinent events, things they had seen, or what they had heard, etc. The basis for the discrepancies was how the human mind, and our defense mechanisms, work. In other words, with the passage of time, sometimes we assuage our perception or recollection of things we have seen or heard in order to allow us to better deal with them internally. It is not lying; it is just human nature; a coping mechanism, so to speak.

Having said that, I do not remember exactly how I accomplished the task of getting Coach Carpenter's *Will* executed in front of two witnesses, an acknowledgment notarized, etc. However, I do know that I got it done, and cannot believe I actually went to Memphis and watched Coach Carpenter sign the document because that is something I think I would vividly remember. A part of me tells me I drove like crazy to Memphis along with my secretary, who was a notary public. Conversely, I have a vague recollection of an intense conversation with some nurse in a supervisory capacity at the hospital with regard to the task at hand, along with instructions as to how to accomplish same. But honestly, I just really, really do not remember, and that perplexes me to this day.

Additionally, after this passage from the *Will* was read by Brother Bob at Coach Carpenter's funeral, I recall there being some consternation among the people present about whether or not Coach Carpenter's body was in the casket, and I felt very bad about the fact that what he had requested, and I had reduced to writing, was a shock to some people who loved him the most. Let me lay the record to rest once and for all. I received a terse, one sentence letter from the surgeon who performed the operation on Coach Carpenter, during which he perished, that read as follows:

> Mr. Boyd:
>   The rigors of surgery rendered Mr. Carpenter's body
> unfit for medical science purposes.

I was glad to get this letter because it got me out of a dilemma. I gave Coach Carpenter my word, under the circumstances spelled out herein, and fulfilled my obligations to him personally, and "legally" based on the attorney/client relationship. I was named the Executor of his Estate in the *Will,* and with that comes certain legal and ethical obligations. However, the *Will* was never admitted to Probate, and we can all be assured that Coach Carpenter was laid to rest, in toto, and without further disturbance.

II

My "Recruitment": What Some Call Fate or Chance, I Call Divine Intervention

Coach Carpenter "recruited" me, along with two hundred fifty other newcomers every year. A "cross-section" of the entire country, along with some who needed passports. We could have had a United Nations meeting. He had a homespun wisdom, wit, and way of dealing with people. Completely unpretentious. He made you feel not only good about yourself, but like he really cared about you and your well-being. For me, that was extremely special, because those of you who know me know that I am not an easy guy to like.[1] For the four years I played for him, he made me feel "at ease," and that what I was doing meant something to him, that I was making a contribution to the team, and had a purpose, guidance, and direction.

When addressing the team, Coach Baker used to always say we were only as strong as our weakest link. That is a good analogy. If I may add another, I feel like a team is akin to a sponge that you squeeze and use to soak up all the good, bad, and "in between" drops of liquid spilt on a table. The "spill" may cover a wide area, and encompass many different kinds and types of "people," but once the sponge soaks it all up, whatever race, color, creed, or area it may be from, becomes irrelevant. When you squeeze the water back out of the sponge, whatever it soaked up has been consumed and diluted, and it comes out as one. I can still hear him say: "Everybody's got to do their own thing." I don't care if you were the president of the United States, the best player on the team, or the person who washed the jock straps, Coach Carpenter spoke to you the same, treated you the same, and made you feel a part of the family.

I do not know how important that is to others reading this book, but to me it was extremely important, and is one of the reasons I will never forget him. It was an innate, genuine, mannerism he possessed. Not a "talent" he had to cultivate. It came natural to him, and was one of his finest attributes. He also liked to use different angles and analogies when addressing the team, with one of his favorite being those players whom he deemed "solid citizens." His favorite example for this category were two genuinely good guys; decent, honest, and dependable in every way: Ted Green and Arvester Brown. I understand one or both of them has been in public school administration for decades now, as you would expect.

Right before a game, Coach Carpenter addressed the team with an intense, yet restrained, passion. You could see the ocean "rise and fall," and feel its "rage and glory" through the "fire in his eyes" as he talked. But, it was contained in a flame thrower, and not turned loose yet. We were told to play with a "controlled frenzy," and a team tends to take on the personality of its coach. He would let loose with a "Gallory Bee!" when a linebacker jacked somebody up, or a running back hit a crease with perfect timing and showed a little "shake and bake" while exploding through the hole. Then he'd grab you by the face mask and start popping you on the side of the helmet while growling at you. Man, you loved it!

I stood a little under 5'7" coming out of high school, and weighed about 160 pounds. To say the least, I was not recruited by anyone as a cornerstone upon which you built your team. But Coach Carpenter tapped into what I believe was a spoonful of competitive spirit and desire, and loyalty, and made me feel like I could somehow make a difference if I parlayed what I had already been taught because I was raised well, and did the best I could in the classroom and on the field. For four years I tried to let people know what the Henderson State University Reddies football team stood for, where we had been, how we expected to be treated when we stepped on our field, or someone else's field, and that we intended to win with dignity, poise, and class. Coach Carpenter always instructed us to forego jumping up and down "like a yo-yo" when we made a big play. "Act like you've been there before." You also never saw a Reddie player get flagged for an undisciplined, unsportsmanlike penalty. "Anybody can act tough when the lights are on."

My hometown, Lake Village, Arkansas, produced an All-American punter/place kicker, Bo ("Easy Livin'") Adkisson. Coach Carpenter had stories that may be mentioned in this book, e.g., the Jasper Benton and Lynn "Stick" Young[2] stories come to mind, that he liked to tell. He was so good at embellishing on them that he was able to get away with it time and time again. He could get away with this tactic because his players, who actually knew he was embellishing, were his captive audience and gladly listened to them over and over. He would tell people that the only reason I came to Henderson State to play football was to carry Bo's kicking tee for him. Now don't get me wrong, I love ol' Bo to death, but the reason I came to Henderson State is actually different.[3] Back in the mid-seventies, the

National Association of Intercollegiate Athletics (the NAIA) had over four hundred fifty teams. Many teams classified as "Mid Major" now were members of the NAIA at that time (which I understand to have since disbanded). After Coach Carpenter had called me a few times on the phone:

> Chally, we just one big family, and we want you to be
> a little part of it.

I came to Henderson State one weekend as a senior in high school and watched us play UAPB. I went from Arkadelphia, to a recruiting visit to UCA (my only other recruiting trip), coached by Ken Stephens (whom I understand will contribute to this book), to the Arkansas State Capitol where I was a "page" for my uncle, Gene Mazzanti Jr., who was a member of the state legislature. By far and away, the highlight of the trip was watching the Reddies.

Back in those days everybody ran the I-formation, with a fullback and a tailback, and only passed when absolutely necessary. But, anyone who has been around football knows that it does not matter what offense you run, the power I or the spread, on third and three you have to be able to double down on the defensive tackle, kick out on the defensive end, run off tackle, make a first down, and move the chains. This keeps your opposing team's offense off the field, and the statistical probabilities of your opponent scoring decrease drastically when its quarterback is a spectator on the sideline. The statistical probabilities of you scoring also go up dramatically when you start at mid-field, instead of your own 20. This occurs when you have a good defense to stop the other team on their end of the field, force a punt, get a decent punt return, and not have as much real estate to cover before you cross the goal line.

I can recall watching how Terry Blaylock "managed" the offense, Lewis Pryor running backward while fielding a punt and going in the opposite direction at full speed in two strides, tailback Joe ("Ho Smif!") Smith pounding it out behind an offensive line ("the Dogs") and fullback Larry "Baby" Ray, a defense that just "smash mouth stuffed" that other team invited to the party, and the Reddies methodically grinding out a victory over an opponent that slowly but surely became demoralized because it was beaten on the fundamentals, a dominating defense, excellent special teams, sound coaching, and a team that believed it would win.[4]

Henderson State lost to an undefeated Texas A & I juggernaut, 34–23 in the National Championship game in 1974, and I was sold on the Reddies.[5]

III
A SNAPSHOT OF MY FOUR YEARS AS A REDDIE, SUPERIMPOSED OVER THIRTY YEARS AS A LAWYER

I was a freshman in 1975, and that was the best athletic team with which I have ever been associated. Defense. Kicking game. And an offense that did not make mistakes and beat itself. That was Coach Carpenter's style, and we were so good at it we were borderline boring to watch.[6] I can still recall OBU beating us 21–20 in the final game my freshman year. That was the only game that year we lost, and on any other day our third team could have beaten them nine times out of ten. We went to the Bicentennial Bowl in Little Rock and beat the winner of the Oklahoma Intercollegiate Conference. That summer we went to Europe and played Texas A & I five times. The purpose of the trip was to stimulate and promote interest in American football in Europe. Think about it. We were a small school in southwest Arkansas doing something that no school or organization, college or professional, had ever done, nor will it likely *ever* be repeated. This feat, was accomplished, and concurrent honor obtained, because of the "program" that had been established by

Coach Carpenter, and because the players on the field *expected* to win. In my four years at Henderson we won thirty-five games, lost seven, and tied one. We won the Arkansas Intercollegiate Conference twice, and were runner up for the conference title the other two years. That ain't bad, based on anybody's math.[7]

But we always felt "unfulfilled." We could never get "over the hump" again and reach the level of excellence defined by the '74 and '75 teams. We went 2–2 against the University of Central Arkansas, which at that time was beginning to outgrow and out-spend the remainder of the conference, and in my opinion replaced Ouachita Baptist as the team we wanted to beat to remain in the class of the AIC. Although we went 2–2 against UCA during my four years, our ability to dominate them as the king of the conference was beginning to wan, and I felt then, and still feel today, like we personally let Coach Carpenter down because we couldn't uphold the same level of excellence and dominance against a larger school, with a larger athletic budget, that was challenging us. This is hard for me to write, and in our defense, I temper same because, to some degree, we were being too hard on ourselves. It was inevitable under the circumstances. But that doesn't take away the sting after thirty years, and I still take it personal. They were on our schedule, and that meant we were *supposed* to beat them. Anything less was a failure. Somewhat akin to the saying among trial lawyers: "You show me a lawyer whose never lost a case, and I'll show you one whose not try-ing lawsuits." But that does not mean you ever *accept* losing.

We started the European tour in Olympic Stadium in West Berlin. We also played in Paris, Vienna, Manheim, and Nuremburg.[8] Games in Rome, Florence, and Genoa, Italy, were canceled while we were in Europe due to the instability of the political climate, which came to a head while we were overseas.[9] After starting in West Berlin we crossed the Brandenburg Gate into East Berlin on our way to Vienna. I can recall the East German border guards checking everyone's passport intently, studying it as they looked at your picture, then you, back and forth, again and again, checking everyone repetitively to make sure that the picture in the passport matched the face of the person holding it. I can remember the eyes of those guards being completely devoid of any human emotion, and leaned over to Ricky Patton, a wide receiver from Camden-Fairview who was a good one (and a great guy) and saying: "Ricky, if one of those guards decides to take one of us off this bus, you're going to find out who your friends are—real quick."

The bus ride through drab, bleak, communist East Germany took eighteen hours. Nonstop. The bus had a governor on it that would not let it travel over forty-seven mph, and for every meal we ate sandwiches with funny tasting meats and that same damn concrete hard bread. Then we got stopped at the border between East Germany and Austria because the check drawn on the NAIA's account to pay the motel bill in West Berlin had bounced. It was 3:00 in the afternoon in East Germany, but 3:00 in the morning in Kansas City, where the NAIA's headquarters were located. Suffice it to say, we could not get anyone out of bed at that time in the morning to put sufficient funds into some account so that the check in question cleared. We were "re-routed" to the American Military Base in Nuremburg, West Germany, and played on the same field where you see the huge Nazi rallies on the Military Channel.

Ricky Minter,[10] a defensive end who (among other stops) later was the defensive coordinator at Notre Dame when Lou Holtz won the National Championship, the head coach at the University of Cincinnati for a decade, the defensive coordinator at South Carolina, and is now the co-defensive coordinator at Kentucky, and I were later in the same Western Civilization class at Henderson, and we spoke about how we wished we had taken the class before going to Europe. Coach Carpenter brought out the poignancy of the moment after practice one day on that very same field,[11] pointing out that we were right in the middle of the huge field where the Nazis and Hitler had their mass rallies, preaching their mindset of racial bigotry, prejudice, and planned retribution.[12] But I don't believe any of us realized the significance at that time. Rick and I didn't. The commander of the United States military base addressed us while we were there. He was a black man, very composed and dignified, yet with an intensity level he portrayed through the fire in his eyes. You could tell he had a lot on his mind. *I mean a lot.* The Cold War wasn't over. Germany and Berlin were still split into "East" and "West." The USSR still existed—along with the anus race and the potential for nuclear Armageddon. Speaking with a "controlled frenzy," I recall him inviting us to bring anything to his attention if he "could make us more comfortable or our stay more enjoyable." But, you could tell we weren't at the forefront of the issues he had to worry about, and rightfully so.

Before I leave this topic behind, I want to state right now that the reason we were able to go to Europe that summer was the 1974 and 1975 teams, and the players on the '74 team and the seniors on the '75 team that did not get to go because they had used up their eligibility. I have always felt bad about that to this day, and to some degree want to apologize to those players, and make sure they know, that we know, that the reason we were invited on that trip was them, and the groundwork they laid before us. For each and every Reddie who was able to make that trip, to each and every member of the '74 and '75 teams, let me take a moment to publicly say what everybody who boarded that plane and crossed the Atlantic Ocean feels, and wishes, they could say— "Thank you."

When I went to Henderson, I had a sister enrolled at the University of Arkansas, who later went to Baylor Dental School in Dallas and became a dentist, a younger sister about to enroll in college at the University of Arkansas and in four years obtain her degree, and a younger brother, who later went to Law School and became an attorney himself in Little Rock prior to passing away from a heart attack this past summer. I was determined that my father was not going to pay my way through college, and let's face it folks, I'm never gonna dunk a basketball. I walked on at Henderson and was honestly grateful I was allowed to share the same dressing room with the players, and on the teams, mentioned herein above.[13] Under the conference rules of the old Arkansas Intercollegiate Conference, each team was allowed thirty-three scholarships, with there being some "finagle" room as to how they were split up.

After two-a-days my sophomore year, I recall Coach Carpenter reading off thirty-three names, and indicating that those individuals had a meeting in his office after practice. It took me by surprise, and honestly was something I did not expect. I had not even lettered my freshman year.[14] But, I instantly "crunched" the numbers of names, realized what that meant, and can tell all of you that regardless of what I might accomplish (in this context anyway) throughout the rest of my life, in the practice of law or otherwise, that day, and that feeling, will top the list.[15] It was not a full scholarship; something I did not obtain until my senior year at Henderson,[16] but I can look back and state that no one ran a wind sprint for me, worked harder in the weight room during the off season for me, nor expended any of the sweat and toil needed and necessary to be in that group.[17] In my office, I have the "Financial Aid Award" framed, front and center, and look at it from time to time when I doubt myself, as we all do.

Henderson Student ID No.: 28972
Soc. Sec. No.: xxx-xx-xxxx
HSU Scholarship: Athletic
Fall 1976: Seventeen hundred and thirty dollars ($1,730.00)
Spring 1977: Six hundred fifty-eight dollars ($658.00)

With the caliber of players around me as teammates, I would

sometimes wonder if I truly belonged on the field with them. Coach Carpenter used to always say something to the effect that:

> If you find yourself out there playing on the field,
> you ain't out there because we feel like you're a great guy.
> You're out there because you're the best we have.

He had a way of predicting things that you as a player, especially one like me who was marginal at best on the talent level/barometer, might be worrying about and putting it to rest before it became a "mental issue." Squelched one of them there "thinkin' things," you know. How many times did we hear him say: "I understand the anxieties that goes through a fella's mind."[18]

I try to use these events in my life by analogy, and as a means to attempt to motivate the young lawyers who work for me.

> I'll provide you with a schedule (i.e., cases to work on and then to be tried to a Judge or Jury);
> A stadium, lights, and facilities (i.e., a furnished office with a support staff, and then the Courtroom);
> Referees for the contest (i.e., the Judges and/or Juries);
> An opposing team that will show up (i.e., your opposing counsel).
> *But, I'm not going to run your wind sprints for you.*

Stated another way, we don't handle speeding tickets, DWI's, or divorces where the parties start arguing over the tupperware. I have never kept a time sheet in thirty years of practicing law. We handle contingency fee cases (which means we fund the cases from start to finish, get a percentage of the recovery, *if* we recover, and eat the costs if we lose) that draw the best defense lawyers in the state as opponents.[19] It can be financially rewarding, or devastating.[20] The "personal toll" this takes on a fella is not for everyone, and the first thing I tell a young lawyer fresh out of Law School with a law degree is that he has a piece of paper he can hang on the wall as decoration. He or she will never make it working forty hours a week, Monday through Friday, and they weed themselves out pretty quickly. No one can pay the "price" for them. The consensus opinion among those lawyers as old as me is that the younger grads are having more and more trouble with this concept.

Another of my coaches, Bradley Mills, awarded "footballs" that players could put on their helmets as decals if they made a big play; e.g., a tackle for a loss, a fumble recovery, a pass interception, hit of the week, etc. We were playing Harding University in Searcy when I was a senior, and it was fourth and goal, with the nose of the football as close to the goal line as it could get. They ran a sweep to my side and I made the tackle for no gain—a gain was not possible without a touchdown. We stopped them and got the ball, and the game ultimately ended in a tie. During the film session on Sunday I asked Coach Mills if I got a "football" for that play, and he said in that calm, cool, monotone voice he had: "Charlie, you don't get a 'football' for doing your job." When a young lawyer completes a task I have assigned to him or her, I use this story and analogy. I thank them for their efforts, but don't give out kudos when they simply do their job.

I cannot rightfully say what would have happened to me had I ended up somewhere else. However, I can say that Henderson State had a system in place, a program that was a proven winner, and a head coach for the ages—Coach Carpenter. He motivated me to be the absolute best I could be, and without him, who knows? He gave me a chance when no one else even provided the opportunity. Anyone that young, regardless of their aspirations or goals, needs others for guidance, and someone they can respect through the ups and downs that will inevitably arise. I wanted to try harder, because of him and for him. Because of him and the foundation laid, prior to a big trial I will always tell those working under me that we might not win, but no one will ever accuse us of being afraid to tee it up and "Run for the Roses." Insurance defense lawyers will never pay a plaintiff's attorney what a case is worth if they think he's afraid to go to trial, and many plaintiff's lawyers are known for "buckling" when it comes down to the lick log.

It's the same concept as the lessons learned, and methods utilized at Henderson, just parlayed into a different arena. We'll tee it up and compete with you, and we will win more often than not just like we did at Henderson, with poise and class, and because we are *supposed* to, expect to, and will *pay* the *price* that has to be paid for you to be in a position to win. The games/trials are fun. But it's the wind sprints you run or your preparation beforehand, that more often than not determines a win or a loss. Ninety-five percent of the "successful/competent" people in a profession, where production and/or performance counts, basically do things the same way. However, those people who will do whatever it takes to nail down the details make up the other 5 percent. (And drive the other 95 percent crazy.)[21] You can spend an infinite amount of time on the details, and the statistical odds are that that which they encompass will never come up in a single game, or single trial, but, over the course of a season, or a career, that extra effort, and those intangibles, elevate the "winners" from those who will spend an entire career being "competent."[22] Coach Carpenter always said: "We ain't gonna be outworked by nobody," and he led by example. We expected to be winners. That was the expected outcome, as much as an accomplishment. When the chips were down, we felt that if we'd just hang in there, and believe in ourselves, something good was going to happen.

That example and attitude has helped me in my career, and in life.

IV
AFTER HENDERSON

I was a typical college graduate in 1979. I could not make up my mind whether I wanted to coach, go to veterinarian science school, go to Law School, go back to Lake Village and farm, or do something else. My boat was totally without a sail or rudder. I had out grown that point in life where you can lean back on your parents, and HSU and Coach Carpenter had done that which they were supposed to do; i.e., made me what Jimmy Jones[23] said a college degree meant you were a "marketable or trainable work in progress, but by no means a finished product." I come from a family of winners who never paid attention to the odds, and for that reason was (and am) also a pretty hardsh self-critic. Due to that up-bringing, and the acceptance and nurturing of that attitude by Coach Carpenter, I expected to work hard enough to be called a winner. Conversely, failure never really entered my mind, as a walk-on at Henderson or an unemployed guy with a piece of paper called a "degree." I knew that paying the "price" was part of the deal, but the issue was: "Where?"

So, I enrolled in Law School in Little Rock, and, after being in the athletic dorm at Henderson for three and one-half years, was miserable in my "new" environment. I recall dropping out of Law School one day at the beginning of my first year and going to the airport here in Little Rock to fly somewhere to be a graduate assistant. My luggage actually went to an out-of-town destination, and, after the last call to board the plane, I was talked out of it at the airport by my father and Coach Carpenter.[24] I re-enrolled in Law School that same day, but immediately drove to Arkadelphia and talked with him late into the evening about what I wanted to do, or what I wanted to be. It was late August, a time when Coach Carpenter was busy getting his own team whipped into shape, yet he took the time to counsel me. Suffice it to say, hindsight is not 20/20 in this instance because I do not know where I would have ended up, nor how far I could have gone elsewhere, if anywhere. However, I do know that I have been practicing law thirty years now, and sometimes feel that is about twenty-nine and one-half too many. But then again, Coach Carpenter used to always say: "It's hell everywhere, boy."[25]

V

ROY GREEN

I could not offer my contribution to this book, and reminisce about the four years I was blessed to play at Henderson State, without mentioning a fellow teammate named Roy Green, from Magnolia.[26] Roy and I played together at Henderson for four years, and he was a phenomenal athlete, by far and away the greatest and most gifted athlete I have ever stepped on the field with. He was definitely a sleeper, and the major colleges missed out when they passed on him. As a fellow player, while on the field with him you had to guard against stopping and just watching him perform magic.

I recall being fortunate enough to be one of the "up backs" on kickoff and punt returns. My job was to call out "green," which meant the return was a go; "red," which meant a fair catch; or another word, which I will not put in this book, which meant to get out of the way and let the ball hit the ground. The most exciting and rewarding thing I got to do while playing at Henderson was being able to block for Roy on kickoff and punt returns. You lined up five yards in front of him as he was fielding the ball, and you could not take a step backward because you would be in his lap. You picked out the first guy wearing a different color jersey, someone who out weighed you by forty pounds and had a forty-yard head start, and hit him so that he did not touch Roy. That was my job, and it brings back the greatest memories I could ever have from college football, being able to block for Roy and making damn sure nobody touched him. If you did that for Roy, and gave him a crease, you were able to watch him from the rear as he took off for the other team's end zone.

One of the greatest compliments ever given to me came from Roy, when he told me one night in the dorm that he had told Coach Mills[27] he wanted me back there with him, regardless of the fact that I "needed some more lead in my ass." Folks, that motivated me to the max. No one wearing a different color jersey touches Roy. No one. The kicking game was very important to our "team concept," our success, and our program, and also gave a lot of guys like me who weren't good enough to start every game a chance to make a contribution. I wish I could have blocked one time for ol' Lewis [Pryor].[28]

Brother Bob was our trainer, and as a licensed minister, our "Chaplain." We said the Lord's Prayer after every game. We would gather around, and Coach Carpenter would say: "Grab a knee, men. Brother Bob, say the Word." We had just beaten Ouachita Baptist the final game of my senior year, 7–6. They had scored on the last play of the game, and then failed on the two-point conversion attempt with no time on the clock.[29] I played a part in breaking up the pass attempt[30] on the play and recall seeing the unmitigated joy on Coach Carpenter's face. The whole stadium, at least everyone who was a Reddie, was ecstatic. We had come around full circle since the bitter one-point defeat my freshman year that knocked us out of the national playoffs and what would have been a rematch with Texas A & I, who had beaten us for the national title in 1974. I was right next to Coach Carpenter when he congratulated OBU's head coach "Buddy Bob" Benson after that loss in '75, and another defeat like that to end my player/coach relationship with him would have been hard to swallow. Conversely, I was right next to Coach Carpenter when we took a post-game team picture with the Battle of the Ravine trophy after the 7–6 victory in 1978. We knew what that game meant to us, to our school, but most importantly, to *him*.

As we gathered around in the dressing room on bended knees for the "Word," I found myself next to Roy. I knew I'd be watching him play on Sundays in the NFL, and reached out, grabbed his hand, and he knew how I felt, and what I meant, as the dialog went as follows:

I'm gonna always be pulling for you, Roy.

Alright, Chally B.

Nothing else needed to be said, then nor now.[31]

Roy played for the St. Louis Cardinals, and still holds the NFL record for the longest kick return in its history—108 yards. I recall watching a game years after Roy had retired when some other player, an imposter who got lucky, returned a kickoff 108 yards, and the commentators on ESPN were calling it an NFL record. That aggravated the hell out of me, and is the only occasion where I have ever taken the time to send an e-mail to the program's announcers, chastising them for taking away a record that was Roy's record, or degrading it by not at least acknowledging that whomever the latter player was that returned his kickoff for 108 yards shared that record with Roy.

Roy was also the last player in the National Football League to play both ways.[32] When Roy was inducted into the Arkansas Sports Hall of Fame, along with Coach Carpenter, his mother accepted the honor in his absence. In her acceptance speech, she made a clarification for the assembled crowd:

> Roy wanted me to make sure everybody knows something. When people say Roy played both ways, that means only on the field.

He was just a good, good guy, a good teammate, a
good person, and a phenomenal talent, athlete, and player.

VI

MY ROOMMATE—PAT LONGINOTTI

I also have to mention my roommate during the years I was at
Henderson, Pat Longinotti. Pat ("Longe") went to Little Rock
Catholic, and most of the time you can tell when someone graduated
from there. Father Tribou instilled a little discipline in the student
population, including Pat.

He and I shared a parochial school background, an Italian her-
itage, and good parents who raised us well. But Pat was also quite a
character; a dual athlete—football and baseball (All-AIC)—with a
pencil-thin mustache. He was the guy in the dorm who had a lot of
personal pranks played on him because he was well liked by everyone, and was quick/easy to share a laugh with you.

Pat and I are still close. To give you a composite example, when
Hurricane Gustav came through Little Rock in September 2008, I
was without electricity for a week. After toughing it out for several
days, I tried to purchase a generator, but the stores had sold out. So I
picked up the phone and called "ol' Longe," and he was at my house
in a matter of hours with a generator, and a priest in his truck who
happened to be staying with him for reasons I can't recall at this time.[33]

In fact, my relationship with Pat is one of those where you can
go years without speaking to someone, and then you can call them
on the phone, see them in person, whatever the circumstances might
be, and it's like you never missed a day. Pick up right where you left
off. Pat is a great guy, and I was fortunate to have him as a roommate.
I would do anything for Pat, at the drop of a hat, if he needed me,
and vice versa. The bond is for life, but I met him at Henderson, and
sweated with him under Coach Carpenter.

VII
My Father's Death

My father passed away on April 12, 2006. He loved football and always enjoyed a conversation with Coach Carpenter. Daddy would drive all the way from Lake Village to Arkadelphia to watch us *practice*. Outside of my father and late brother, Joel, two good as gold brothers-in-law, Ed and Harvey, several of my favorite uncles, and a lawyer here in Little Rock, Bud Whetstone,[34] there is not a man in my life I love, nor respect, more than Coach Carpenter, nor one who has had as much of an impact on my life. He surfaced during a conversation on a day a son will never forget.

Several days before my father went to heaven, we were all waiting for a priest to arrive to administer the Last Rites of the Catholic Church. Jerry Mazzanti, one of three of my uncles who played for the Arkansas Razorbacks (and later a decade or so in the NFL), and I were talking in the hospital's critical care visitors' room in Greenville, Mississippi, and the parallels between the coaches and the fathers that athletes have had in their lives became the topic of conversation. I remember telling him how Coach Carpenter's players felt about him and would do *anything* for him. An example I used was that if he had told me to go sit on the railroad tracks, face down and without looking up, it did not matter how many times the train blew its horn, I was safe and secure because I knew Coach Carpenter would never tell me a lie nor do anything to hurt me. Uncle Jerry, who has a heart as big as he is, in a moment that an uncle, nephew, and two former players could share without having to fill in all the gaps between the lines, drew a comparison between Coach Carpenter and one of his coaches at the University of Arkansas, Wilson Matthews. He spoke about how Coach Matthews loved his players, and the affection and bond that existed between them. Because of that conversation, I know Coach Matthews without ever meeting him, and because of Coach Carpenter he's a special man.

My father is the greatest man I have ever known in my life, and I'm the most fortunate man in history to have had him for as long as I did.[35] He was raised by a single mother who worked for over forty years as a nurse on the night shift at King Daughter's Hospital in Greenville, Mississippi. He overcame his own adversity, yet always had the time to help me overcome mine whenever needed, or necessary, as a boy and after I reached the "age of majority." He gave me the blueprint for an overachiever, and it's in my blood to take up the cause for the underdog. I accept my role as a plaintiffs' trial lawyer, standing up for the common folks who have been injured or damaged, in front of a jury of twelve people representing a cross-section of society, who would otherwise have no voice, nor means to seek redress.

My maternal grandparents were Italian immigrants who came to America and prospered here due to the respect they earned through hard work and familial values. My mother was one of eleven children, and, being the next daughter born, was named after her two sisters who had drowned while taking a bath in Lake Chicot because their house had no running water. Together my parents raised four children who all obtained college degrees in four years[36] with two going on to become attorneys here in Little Rock, one a practicing dentist in Dallas and mother of three of five of the best kids around, and one, married to a dentist in Fayetteville, who raised two fine children.[37]

When I was a sophomore at Henderson, Coach Carpenter spoke at my former high school's athletic banquet in Lake Village. We had driven there together from Arkadelphia that afternoon, and we went to my parents' house afterward and visited with them later that evening. We were all as comfortable as a newborn baby sleeping in a warm cotton quilt.

Good people know good people when they meet them. They communicate well because they have the same foundation and share common traits. My father was happy to "loan" me to Coach Carpenter for four years, and, after completing spring practice at Henderson in 1976, he told me: "I want you to know I'm proud of you" on a Sunday afternoon when I was home for the weekend, just before I drove back to Arkadelphia. There was no audience; we were alone. No one jumped up and down like a "yo-yo"; we both acted like we had "been there before." It was where a father and son expected to be because a winner (my dad) had raised a son striving to get there. Simply put, it wasn't taken for granted, but the world was "as it should be," and we handled it with "poise, dignity, and class," the same way the Reddies handled themselves. Daddy also knew Coach Carpenter was the "custodian" to whom I was entrusted, and to whom I was returning, and that I was in good hands.

CONCLUSION

The title of this book is a classic "Sportyism." We had just gotten beat by UAM at their place, and the "dressing room" for the opposing team was around an indoor pool. I recall being next to Coach Carpenter when the reporter asked him what happened, and can attest, under oath, that his answer was just what the title of this book says it was. For all of his players who loved him, and remember him, there will never be another. He lives on within each of us. I beg to differ with those of you who believe our lives are etched in stone when we exit the womb and that you can't change fate. When I went to Henderson State, and my life interfaced with Coach Carpenter, "lightning struck it," because he epitomized those traits in a man that are at the top of the list. Traits that can remain dormant for long periods of time, especially if we *let* them, but we have to strive every day to keep them alive. I don't always do the right thing, but because of my family and him, I know it, and feel it instantly in my heart, when I fall short. Hard work. Decency. Honesty. Dedication. Duty. Loyalty to your family, to your school, your coaches, your colors, and, above all, to your teammates. Those who came before you, those who sweated blood in the same mud with you, and those who carry the banner after you.

Let us endeavor to be "Living Legacies to the Leader of the Band," and save a chorus of that "Old Time Religion" for the Pearly Gates.

I love you, Coach. We all love you. And, from the bottom of our hearts, we all thank you.

NOTES

1. The playing field at Henderson's Carpenter-Haygood Stadium was recently taken up, and Astro Turf was installed. I made it a point to secure some of the old "sod" for a keepsake/souvenir. "Spilt blood in that mud," you know. Some folks would call that eccentric. The house next door to me recently sold, and my new neighbors moved in one weekend. They are a nice family; husband and wife, with two small children. We are told that we never get a second chance to make a first impression, and, on a Sunday afternoon, this young mother is watching me water and meticulously groom this clump of grass in an old, rusty, plant canister. I attempted to explain to her why this small, rectangular piece of sod was important to me, and could tell by the look on her face that I was never going to get there. I've now got a lot of "rehabilitating" to do in order to save, if possible, my sanity in her eyes. Don't tell her I've got a chunk of concrete from Goodloe on my coffee table.

2. Coach Carpenter taught drivers' education, and he could converse with the student/driver through the vehicle's audio speakers, and/or loud-speakers set up in the parking lot (the classroom), which had an obstacle course set up with those orange cones. Lynn had a "love/hate" relationship when he drove the course, and as he sheepishly grinned from ear to ear, Coach Carpenter loved to fatherly boom out: "Faster, Lynn, faster, makes those wheels squeal. *Squeal,* Lynn, squeal!"

3. When I was a sophomore in high school, four members of our track

team came to the "Reddie Relays," and that asphalt/synthetic track was pretty awesome to a boy from Lake Village whose "track" was a dirt patch around the football bleachers. I had also met Coach Carpenter, who served as a counselor at Boys' State, during the summer between my junior and senior years in high school, and instantly knew he had the ability to sell ice cream to an Eskimo. I scored high enough on one of those aptitude tests the U.S. military gives all high school seniors to receive a scholarship to the U.S. Naval Academy in Annapolis, but the war in Vietnam was raging then, and with it the battering of the psych of America's youth. I don't think there's any finer achievement than being a U.S. Navy Seal, and, but for the evolving tragedy of Vietnam, and the connection I made with Coach Carpenter, I sometimes wonder what it would be like to have the "SEAL Trident," popularly nicknamed "The Budweiser," on your mantel.

4. My sophomore year we went 8–2. However, a trademark statistic from that year is that our defense shut out eight teams. One team was awarded a safety when we punted out our end zone. The center snapped the ball high, causing Bo to jump for it, and his back foot came down on the back end zone line. Those were the only points "scored" by our opponent that game. Another fast fact about football: It is impossible to lose a game if your opponent fails to score.

5. Coach Carpenter had me locked up from day one tighter than a tick on a dog. Truthfully, I had no where else to go and didn't have the cards to play "hard to get with a poker face." But he called me one day to seal his "recruiting coup," and said the "HSU Administration" had had a cancellation on one of those academic scholarships based on an applicant's ACT score, and that I had been "awarded" a $250 tuition scholarship. I was sly and led him on for a while, telling him I was "on the fence," trying to decide between Henderson, Texas, USC, and Alabama, but eventually capitulated and "committed" to the Reddies on the spot. Stated another way, I was "important" enough to warrant a phone call from him, and it didn't matter if we both knew; he was just letting me feel like I controlled my own fate.

6. Coach Russell Cerratto, our offensive coordinator my freshman year, was the consummate stickler for details, and demanded repetitions in practice until you got your footwork right.

7. Skip Davidson bought me an engraved Rolex watch on the tenth year anniversary of my employment at his law firm, and it is/was sincerely appreciated. My only other piece of jewelry is our 1977 "AIC Champs" ring, with the words "Time Takes All But Memories" under a sun dial with roman numerals etched into the outside, and my name engraved on the inside. I have a tendency to misplace things, everything, all the time. I can

misplace my Rolex and get by just fine for a while with my $9.95 Casio from Walmart. But if I can't find that ring, the world stops turning until I do.

8. Our "accommodations" ran the gauntlet. We stayed in a boarding-house for lost children in West Berlin, and ate ("Grease your Gums" as Coach Carpenter would say) concrete hard rolls with some awful form of minestrone soup with a German "twist," and then a luxury motel in Vienna with veal parmesan. We found a McDonald's in one city, and acted like five-year-olds at Christmas waiting in line for the Big Macs. Vienna was the prettiest. I still remember the different colored tulips in the medians between the streets. Paris was pretty also; the Champs-Elysees, Arc de Triomphe, Cathedral at Notre Dame, and the street-side cafes. The liters of European beer, and the ice cream vendors, were everywhere, in every city. Finally, I predicate this last observation with the fact that I like classic rock and not classic symphonies, but the smile on the Mona Lisa never tweaked an inquisitive bone in my body. She looks the same in your history books as she does in the Louvre.

9. For those of you who are history buffs, this unrest finally led to the abduction and later assassination of the country's prime minister, Aldo Moro, by a communist political sect known as the Red Brigades. His body was found several years later in Rome on May 9, 1978, stuffed in the trunk of a car. I remember reading about the events in *Time* magazine and relating them back to the summer of 1976.

10. If you could draw up a blueprint for a coach, it would be Rick. He played from his shoulders up. Rick got out of coaching for a while and came to Little Rock to work as a broker in the investment business. He, Dan Harshfield, and I would go to the Sports Page, a burger joint, for lunch, and Rick would start diagraming plays with the ketchup bottle and salt and pepper shakers. Man, he was "ate up" with coaching. You always knew he would get back in it, and I hope he's happy doing what he loves.

11. Coach Carpenter was fiercely competitive and could not stand mediocrity. We never beat Texas A & I, but every game was close, real close. If we had a two-hour segment of time not spent on a bus, drinking beer, or asleep, we practiced, and practiced, in full pads ("full regalia") every day on that trip. No one complained; it was expected and treated as business as usual. You also turn eighty-eight college kids (forty-four for each team) loose in huge European cities, often telling them they must use other "liq-uids" to stay hydrated because the water is bad, plus the fact that the European's view of what Americans see as taboo is a little lax, and—you guessed it—a few beers were consumed. One day a few players were late to practice with hangovers, and I can still see Coach Carpenter standing up

in the front of the bus and bellowing out: "Hell, I figured ya'll would go out and have a few beers, but I never thought you'd try to soak up the whole damn town." But, folks, in our defense, we were nineteen years old, and, well, boys will be boys. We like to ride our horses and shoot our guns.

After a month of spring football in full pads, three weeks of extra practice in May, also in fall pads, to get ready for our trip in June, and five games in twenty-one days against the '74, '75, and eventual '76 National Champions, we returned to the States at the end of June beat up, dead legged, and dead tired. We opened the '76 season in August against East Central Oklahoma in Ada on national TV, were extremely lackluster, going through the motions, yet still won 9–0. Coach Carpenter did not like that *at all*. "Brutal." The coaches had taken it "easy" on us when we reported for two-a-days prior to the game so we could "heal from our trip," but we had an open date before our next game, and Coach Carpenter found out who wanted to play. We ran wind sprints you couldn't add up with a calculator, and heat Arkansas Tech 28–0 the next game. Tech had a big fullback who was running all over us until Robert ("The Hump") Hester, a linebacker from Clarendon, laid him out over on our sidelines with a "de-cleater" where the first thing that hit the ground was the back of his head. Tech's trainers hauled him off as a casualty of war, and the game was over.

12. The seeds for Germany's unrest, and the political climate that ultimately "inspired" a civilized people to allow themselves to be led to ruin, were actually sown at the Treaty of Versailles, ending WWI, which totally, unfairly, and entirely blamed the German people for the war, and buried them in a sea of financial debt and national degradation. When France surrendered to Germany twenty-five years later, during WWII, Hitler made it sign its capitulation in the same railroad boxcar where the Treaty of Versailles was executed, then blew it up, consummating France's humiliation. "Sympathy for the Devil," by the Rolling Stones, is actually a trip through history with the Devil, with pertinent lyrics as follows: "Rode the tank, in the General's rank, when the blitzkrieg reigned, and the bodies stank" (The Holocaust).

13. I had the best technique in the conference for holding blocking dummies.

14. I remember the team meeting the night before the first game my sophomore year when a list of the freshman lettermen from the previous season were called out and my name was not on it. It almost killed me. I had been touched by the blanket ceremony for the preceding year's seniors, and could see the letter "H" on my letterman's jacket and senior blanket only having three, instead of four, bars on it. I recall asking Coach Mills in anguish: "Why? *Why?* I played as much as the other freshmen who lettered.

Now, no matter what I do, or how hard I work, I can *never* make up for this." Coach Carpenter was very sick and had not attended this meeting, which meant he had to be almost dead, yet he came up to the dorm that night and talked to me about it for a long, long time. He explained to me why the other freshmen had lettered, one by one, instead of me, and said: "Chally, I don't want you to think that you weren't considered, and that we didn't talk about it. I want to make sure the cobwebs in your head are cleared up. You ain't been ostracized." Every former player can see him saying what he said to me, and how he said it. When he left that night, my mind was at ease. On December 8, 2005, my house burned down at 2:00 a.m. when the chimney flue caught on fire, taking with it my letterman's jacket and the senior blanket my father had draped over my shoulders on November 17, 1978, at the blanket ceremony for those players who were seniors with me. That killed me, again.

15. About twenty-five of the scholarships were "spoken for" every year, and then you had about two hundred players competing for the remaining eight. Some players couldn't stay on the team, as a matter of finances, or wouldn't stay, as a matter of pride, if they didn't get a "ship." When my name was called out, I recall grabbing the shoulder pads of a great guy whom I will not name and saying spontaneously: "I got a scholarship, man! *I got a scholarship!*" I could tell by the look on his face that he had not made the list, and, to this day, felt I inadvertently came across as insensitive, and that has bothered me. I wish I knew where he was now, and have thought about trying to look him up to apologize. But then again, he's undoubtedly prospered in life in ways where I've fallen short. I was also one of those guys who had to earn his scholarship *every year*, which fortunately I did, and would have rather taken a dagger to the heart than give up my "ship."

16. On the day of my senior year when scholarships were awarded, I was at Coach Carpenter's office first thing in the morning. Although he knew full well why I was there, he asked me with a look of surprise on his face: "What are you here for, Chally?" I just looked at him and didn't say a word. Then with a chew of tobacco in his mouth, while bent over that trash can, he said: "Well, I'll tell you what's gonna happen, Chally, Tim Boyd [another player, no relation] is gonna beat your ass out." Coach Baker had come to the doorway, overheard the conversation, and with a chuckle said: "Chally [when Coach Carpenter christened you, it stuck] didn't get up this early in the morning to hear that." Coach Carpenter then signed the paper for me to take to the registrar's office, indicating I had received a final scholarship.

17. As a freshman, I asked a lot of irrelevant questions during film sessions, trying to somehow make myself appear relevant. It aggravated the

hell out of everybody, including Baby Ray, and nobody wanted to aggravate Baby. Every year when we reported as a team, the first thing the coaches did was put us through a battery of tests. One of them consisted of the 180-yard shuttle run, which consisted of two orange cones—one at the starting line and one 60 yards down field. You had to circle the far one, come back and circle the one at the starting line, then do a 180° turn on a dime and sprint through the opposite cone at the finish line. The potential "secret" pitfall: If you "touched" one of the cones you had to do it over, and Coach Baker (who had the stop watch and was a stickler for details like this) loved to be the bearer of this bad news. If a player unknowingly "touched" one of those cones, Coach Baker withheld this information until he finished the entire course, thus ensuring that he was not robbed of the pleasure of running the *entire* course—*again*. Well, when I was a senior, Coach Baker apprised me that I had "nipped" one of the cones—after I had completed the course, of course. Starting from a dead stand still to full speed, then starting up again to a full sprint, three times, was very, very hard. After my "second" shuttle run, I was on my knees, losing my breakfast, while the rest of the team was going into the locker room. Baby Ray, who was then a graduate assistant, was helping me up and I could hear Coach Carpenter hollering out in a voice that resonated through an empty stadium built into a horseshoe: "Hey, Chally, you got any questions?" For four years, every time I bumped into Coach Carpenter, he would greet me the same way: "You got any questions, Chally?" If he saw me walking across campus a mile away, he'd bellow out the same thing from that gray "Reddie" pick-up truck he always "tooled" around in. "Hey, Chally, you got any questions?"

18. I was closer to 5'7" than 5'6", and at that age it was a real big deal to me to be given the benefit of the higher number when it was "rounded off" in the football program, or anywhere else. Roy Green missed the final game of my sophomore year due to an illness, and as the fifth defensive back, I got to "start" my first game at Henderson. At that time, HSU "allowed" OBU to share this date as a joint Homecoming game ("whatsoever you do for the least of my brothers . . ."). I got one of the programs to keep as a souvenir, and saw where I was listed at 5'6". I drew up the courage to go to Coach Carpenter's office and ask him if the programs could be re-printed to list me at 5'7". He could see that it was important to me, and, after making some phone calls on my behalf, reported that all the programs had been printed, and could not be recalled. I was insistent, and I can see him leaning over that trash can in his office with a chew of tobacco in his mouth: "Chally, don't you understand the damn program's done been printed. Next year, I promise I'll have you listed at 6'2" if you

want." At least once during game week over the next three years, he'd sneak up behind me, goose me on the butt, and then wink at me and say: "Checked the program, Chally, and guess what, you're 5'7" this week."

19. Coach Carpenter used to always say, "We don't play patsies."

20. Another Sportyism: "You can go from chicken to feathers, boy, at the drop of a hat."

21. "Chally, I'll say one thing for you, you do take care of your details."

22. As you get older, you see people who are successful and realize that there are parallels between, but also different paths taken by, those individuals. When I passed the Bar, I had no idea where I was going to get a job, or how. But when faced with a dilemma, I drew upon something that had always worked. I ran a few wind sprints. I made about forty copies of a pretty inconspicuous resume and started going floor to floor in every high-rise building in downtown Little Rock. When I saw the words "Attorney-at-Law" on a door, I'd walk in, hand them a copy of my resume, shake their hand, and say: "My name is Charlie Boyd. I just passed the Bar and need a job. You can let me work for a month at no pay, and if you don't like what you get you can fire me—no questions asked." Coach Carpenter and former HSU president Marvin Garrison were two of my references, and they helped me land a job with Skip Davidson, who was from Lake Village of all places. I practiced law with Skip for over eighteen years, and to this day can't see how he stomached being under the same roof with me for that length of time. Skip is a great guy and a damn good lawyer, but his best traits were two he shared with Coach Carpenter: Number 1 is his work ethic (both of them used to always say: "You gotta be willing to pay the price."), and number 2 his ability to tap into someone's individual talents and let them run with it, as long as they stayed within the system. Skip and I never had a major disagreement or argument. Whenever we'd discuss splitting up a fee we'd joke that men argue over two things: Women and money. We never argued over a woman, and amicably resolved any money issues. I would often go into his office and, after discussing an issue, walk out asking: "How did he get me to agree to that? With a smile?" I tell him to this day he reminds me of how former British prime minister Margaret Thatcher (the "Iron Lady") described her meetings with the former head of the Soviet Union, Mikhail Gorbachev: "He's a nice man with a nice smile. But he does it through iron teeth." I had a certain amount of success starting out as a trial lawyer, taking the cases nobody else wanted, and had several opportunities/offers to go to work for other law firms, both in state and elsewhere. This naturally got back to Skip, and one day he simply said: "Charlie, we hope you stay," to which I responded: "Skip, you gave me a chance to practice law in Little Rock when nobody else would, and I owe

you something. I'm not going anywhere." It hurts me to not see that same loyalty returned by a lot of young lawyers, and people in general, nowadays. Skip and Coach Carpenter are/were both decent, honest, intelligent, hard working, *loyal,* and highly successful; paternally influential on me for reasons that are different in a lot of ways, yet the same in many.

23. One of my professors at Henderson and the type of teacher a student needs to be exposed to while in college, Jimmy was a former coach, a south Arkansas "Confucius" with a quick wit, and somewhat of a free spirit. Blessed with the ability to deliver, on the spot, a psychological analogy to the set of circumstances within which you might find yourself at a particular moment. I can still hear him lecturing in class: "People say you're supposed to wear your watch on your left hand. Why? Same thing goes for your ring. Hell, it's yours. Wear it on your nose if you want to." He was also accommodating to students, during hours or for an ear at night if you needed one, and would give you the benefit of the doubt on the answer to a question on an exam if you could show him where the textbook left room for equivocation. "You got to get 'cognitive' on the subject," he'd say. He was also a pallbearer at Coach Carpenter's funeral, and had tears rolling down his cheek during the service. Poignant "drops" from that "team sponge" used by way of illustration earlier.

24. The truth be known, I'm the exact opposite of a "live and let live" guy, and Coach Carpenter knew that. I overanalyze things when I'd be better off just pulling the trigger. Caution can be good, as long as it's not crippling. Coach Mills told me one time: "Charlie, you worry about what to do sometimes when a week from now it's not gonna make a damn bit of difference." Coach Carpenter played the Devil's advocate with me numerous times with regard to the pros and cons of coaching. The summer between my first and second years of Law School we again had some conversations about me being a graduate assistant, this time for Monty Kiffin, who had gone from the UAF to North Carolina State and took Rick Minter with him, but he could never seal the deal for me because I couldn't make up my mind. Finally, he said: "Chally, you'd be a good coach because you had to play sound and smart due to your size limitations, but why don't you stop torturing yourself mentally, and just join the navy like I did. At your age, hell it don't make a damn bit of difference what you do for the next three years."

25. Several years after I graduated I feel like I let Coach Carpenter down, and now I need to get something off my chest. The Reddies were undefeated and ranked No. 1 in the country, and Coach Carpenter called me up and asked me to come down and address the team. His request was seconded by Coach Mills. Well, the long and short of the story is I was

"too busy" to take the time to drive from Little Rock to Arkadelphia, and, honestly, didn't think there was anything I had to say that was really worth hearing. I chose instead to send a letter, which was read to the team on Friday night, and the next day we got beat. Coach Baker tells me Coach Carpenter never held it against me, and I know that's true, but it's one of those things in life where you don't get a second chance to do the right thing in the first place.

26. While our offensive scheme was methodical, our punt and kickoff returns were electrifying. We used to say we had two offenses at Henderson, Lewis Pryor and then our regular offense, and, after Lewis hung up his cleats, Roy Green followed by our regular offense.

27. Coach Mills, our defensive backs/coordinator and special teams coach, had been a roommate of Howard Schnellenbecker, the coach widely credited with reviving the football program at the University of Miami, when they were teammates at the University of Kentucky. He had tremendous knowledge of the game, and was the best X's and O's coach I ever played under, or, for that matter, heard provide "color cornmentary/expert analysis" on ESPN. Years later, and unbeknown to me for some time, he died of a heart attack cooking a steak on his patio. His wife, Madge, called my office one day and left a message I did not timely return. When I finally learned of his death, I tried to reach her and was unable to do so. I have always felt bad about that, and, Madge, if you read this, please accept my sincere apology.

Upon further reflection, she might want to still ring my neck after Coach Mills agreed to keep a lab puppy I obtained while at Henderson because he had a new litter from his dog at his house. We thought they'd all be one, big, homogenous family. That didn't last but one night. My puppy yelped all night, and I had to retrieve my "retriever" and make other arrangements immediately. Dr. Clyde Berry, a former baseball coach at Henderson who was still a professor there at the time and as fine a man as you'll ever meet in your life, lived in a house right next to campus and tried keeping that puppy for a while. He was as gracious as one could ever be about it, but that didn't work out, either. My father picked the puppy up one night after the next home game at Henderson and brought him to Lake Village. I kept three generations of "pick of the litter" descendants from that dog over a period of time that well exceeded thirty years, and always thought of how they allowed me to hold onto a little piece of Henderson, and Coach Carpenter, every time I petted them.

28. Lewis was one of Coach Carpenter's favorites and is one of those guys who just looks like a football player. Square jawed, high cheekbones, with a squint of piss and vinegar in his eyes. He went to camp with the

New Orleans Saints, and made it until the last cut. Lewis was a senior on the '74 team discussed herein, and I can't tell you how hard I was pulling for him. I liked ol' Lewis even before he paid my plane fare to Europe, and enjoy bumping into him every chance I get. Coach Carpenter used to always lament: "I wish I could go out and find me some more Pryors and Grosses" (Johnny Gross, a damn good defensive lineman and fella; he and Lewis were both from Camden).

29. I'll never forget locking eyes with Chester "the Molester" Barnes, a linebacker from Camden, when they scored. Chester and I were freshmen together and were present for OBU's infamous 21–20 last-minute victory (debacle) in 1975. But, we weren't thinking *deja vu*. The telepathic communication was as clear as if we had shouted it in the other's ear. "This ain't gonna happen again."

30. Ned Parette, a linebacker from Fayetteville, somehow stole the credit for the play, and never passed up a chance to "rib" me about it. Ned was quite a character, but also a good guy, and a damn good player.

31. Every spring, we had pro-scouts come to Henderson and "evaluate" all the college players who had used up their eligibility. You would get a call from Coach Carpenter, and have to go down to the field house, dress out, have your height and weight recorded, get timed in the 40-yard dash, etc. . . . I called Coach Carpenter one day and said: "Coach, you know I'll do anything for you, and if you ask me to keep doing this, I will. But we both know I'm not going to play pro football on Sundays, and I would rather be spending my time doing something else." His response: "Well, Chally, I done promised them boys that every player I had that was eligible for the draft would be evaluated, and in order to keep them coming back, you probably need to do that for me." So I did. One day one of the scouts was measuring my height, and the scene was kind of funny to both of us because I was standing up on my tiptoes a little bit and joking with him about it. He told me with a chuckle to "be still," because he was trying to give me the "benefit of the doubt," and to which I responded: "Now you better give me 5'7", or you're going to knock me down from a low first round pick to a late third rounder." I waited by the phone all day on Draft Sunday and never got the call. I know it's because that scout listed me as just over 5'6", instead of 6'7". Let me tell you from experience folks, no matter how much time you spend in the weight room, you can't make your legs grow.

32. Roy played wide receiver and defensive back because of his exceptional talent. This was decades after the days of normal single platoons, leather helmets, Model T's, Pearl Harbor, etc.

33. During this period of time, I was handling a case against Batesville

Casket Company with Tommy "Too Tough" Thrash, who was a defensive back for OBU from 1972 through 1975. The gravamen of the lawsuit was that Batesville Casket manufactured and marketed caskets through the years that were "guaranteed" to be "completely resistant to the entrance of air, water, and graveside elements" for a period of forty years. In other words, waterproof. The truth is their guarantee is a complete fraud. The problem is no one digs up Momma to find out they've been lied to. Tommy called me up at 9:00 one night, as I was floundering in the dark, and invited me over to stay with him, his wife, Toni, and his bulldog T-Bone. He had a serious breakdown in judgment when he decided to go to OBU, but has recovered now to the point that he is a good friend, a fine man, and a great lawyer.

34. Outside of my family, Bud took Coach Carpenter's place. Unpretentious. Honest. And Loyal. He sends me cases from time to time, and, unlike a lot of lawyers, instead of having a set "referral fee" arrangement, we use what Bud calls the "do right" rule. We take into account the complexity of the case, the amount of the recovery, the time, effort, and costs necessary to secure any recovery, whether or not I have to personally and financially commit to, prepare for, and endure a tough trial (what Bud calls a "slobberknocker"), and all other attendant facts and circumstances. In the past, Bud has deferred, indefinitely, payment of a referral fee for various reasons, but he knows it'll come, in due course. That's trust, folks, and the world could use a little more. And then there is friendship. Psychologists say you get attached to your pets because they provide continuity through the ups and downs of life. I can't say I am closer to many men than I am my dog, but Bud has been my best friend through the best and bleakest of times and is a "teammate" for life. I'd jump in the foxhole with him when the shells are coming in, and vice versa.

35. The most important thing about the way you spell my name is the last two letters; i.e., Charles Phillip Boyd, "**Jr.**" I love you, too, Momma, but this is a guy thing. Okay?

36. Now we weren't "poor" by any means, but were raised to be frugal, when necessary, and to take pride in working an honest day for an honest dollar. That should have come across to the reader by now as a characteristic my parents shared with Coach Carpenter. He told me one time: "Chally, you done had to work so hard for everything you've got, it's done made you hard as a rock on the inside." I took that as one hell of a compliment.

37. "There ought to be a Hall of Fame for mommas."

Cliff Garrison

I had been the head junior high coach at Wynne—football, basketball, and track, it was my first coaching job. When the high school job opened up after that first year, I applied for the job. The superintendent was wise enough to not give me the job. I didn't know who they would bring in and, of course, they hired Sporty to be the head football coach. He came in and brought Spriggs Nutt as basketball coach. They moved me up from junior high to assistant senior high basketball and assistant football coach and assistant track coach. Little did I know when I met Sporty how our relationship would last through the years. I had been under some great coaches in my career and played for some great coaches, but I certainly didn't know the education I was going to get in that one year with Sporty.

At that time Wynne was not a power house to say the least. We were going through a rough time and Sporty came in with a lot of enthusiasm and, of course, he was so organized. I was amazed at his organization. He had his plays all put in these plastic binders and things. I was a single guy and Spriggs was a single guy so we just kind of lived and breathed the coaching, which was right down Sporty's alley.

We got into the season and it wasn't going that good, but we did win our first ball game; we beat Newport two to nothing. Coming back on the bus we were talking and we thought we had it going! Sporty would come by our apartment on Saturday morning, you didn't practice much then on Saturdays, and get Spriggs and me and take us down to the local coffee shop to talk to the "wolves," as he called them. He would say, "Hey, we're going down to the coffee shop to face these SOBs," or whatever. To me that was unusual, I had always heard of coaches avoiding the fans, especially after a loss, but Sporty was going to embrace them and that's what we did.

That first morning after the Newport win he said, "Yeah, we beat them as bad as we could, two to nothing."

So we go along there and we don't win another game that year, actually, we tied one and that was it. But, we continued to go down to the coffee shop and face the wolves, and if something happened in the game to turn the tide against us, and the fans would ask, "What happened, coach?" Sporty would say, "Bad breaks and crooked referees will beat you every time!" Of course, they would just laugh and the situation would be defused. Or he would say, well, you are going to have to ask Cliff, he coached the offense or you are going to have to ask Cliff, he coached the defense, depending on which way it worked.

So we go through the season and had only won one game, he came by to get us to go to the coffee shop and I didn't want to go, but he said, "Come on, we're going down there and face them." So he said, "Cliff and I were talking and we decided that we didn't have such a bad year after all." Of course, someone asked how he figured that one victory and one tie and eight losses wasn't such a bad year. Sporty said, "Well, we won one, we tied one and we got upset eight times!"

I learned a lot about how to handle adversity and nobody worked harder than we did. It didn't make any difference what happened, we would come back and we would work, work, work! We would get there early and work all day! He was amazing, when someone tried to cut him, verbally, he would always come back with something.

Clyde Berry
Former head football and baseball coach at Henderson State

Author's note: I had the opportunity to interview Dr. Clyde Berry after a Reddie Hall of Honor meeting on the Henderson State campus April 29, 2009. Dr. Berry is a man of incredible stature! He has many honors following his name. Clyde Berry is a competitor in every sense of the word. I am unable to adequately describe the breadth and depth of this man because of my poor grasp of the written word. Before I unintentionally make this book a tribute to this worthy man, let me just say that Dr. Clyde Berry is an old school coach who was and is and will always be "coach," to several generations of young men who left his company the better for their association with this truly great mentor. He was the highly successful head baseball and football coach for the Reddies on separate occasions. He holds the distinction of having the best record in Reddie football history. The following is my transcription of that interview.

DR. BERRY

I did not know Sporty Carpenter until I had gone to Wynne to recruit. Sporty was head football coach at Wynne and that day I was so impressed with him and how he felt about boys. His excitement and motivation, his whole make up, made me think immediately, "Hey, I might ought to consider this guy as an assistant coach. I came back and talked to Coach Wells about him and of course, Coach Wells said, "Yes, go get him if he will come." So, I got Sporty and I got Donaldson (Charley Donaldson, at that time the only Reddie to have made All-American) and those two solidified my staff. I was also fortunate to hire Bill Hoskins. Hoskins was a very intelligent individual who knew the game. Even though he wasn't a Reddie, I knew him from being a Stuttgart boy. He graduated from UCA. He and Donaldson hit it off real well and Sporty and I hit it off real well. I never had to even consider the defense; I knew Donaldson and Hoskins could do it! I always refer back to the very first day we had our first staff organizational meeting, Sporty and I went together and, of course, Hoskins and Donaldson went together. The only thing Sporty and I did the whole day was to organize the huddle! I came back later and told the staff, "Hey, that's where the offense starts. If you don't have organization in the huddle, you are not off to a good start."

Sporty had all the qualities that you look for in an offensive line coach, because the kids loved him, he was a great motivator, of the four main categories of football, offensive line, offensive backs, defensive line, defensive backs, the hardest to motivate is the offensive line. Sporty had that quality. They got their motivation and they got their accolades from Sporty. They appreciated him, he was a father figure, a big brother figure, anything you want to say, and he just had those qualities. He made a great impact, not only on the kids he coached, but he made a great impact on this university. He really did, he picked up the spirit of the whole university. There are so many things that Sporty did that most people don't realize. He had a great rapport with the administration. I didn't have that. Sporty had the support of the whole administration and I felt that he had the support of the faculty. I was so fortunate to have the staff I had here.

Everything I asked Sporty to do was done without supervision; he took a large load off the mind of the head coach. I put him in charge of equipment, buying, fitting, all aspects of equipment, I knew that what I asked him to do was going to be done and done well.

D. C. Macdonald

The one thing I remember Coach Carpenter always saying to me was, "D. C., you need to get your little ass over to the trough and grease your gums. We gotta get some weight on you, boy." The one ongoing story that became legend was about Coach Carpenter having a weather machine in his office that had buttons for "HOT," "HOTTER," and "RAIN ON THE PARKING LOT." Coach Carpenter gave me an opportunity that many other coaches would not because of my size. I think he knew that I was a big man trapped in a little man's body. I will always be grateful to him for that opportunity because it was the foundation that I have built my coaching career on. My athletes always ask me where I come up with all the crazy sayings that come out of my mouth and the majority of them are attributed to Ralph "Sporty" Carpenter.

Dale "Mutt" Diemer
> Teammate at Henderson

I played football with Sporty at Henderson. I graduated in 1955 so I was a year or so ahead of him. I started to Henderson in the fall of 1948. I attended for three semesters and went into the service. He and I played the same position. He sure made it tough on me because he would fire up the defensive players and encourage them to play extra tough against the particular group he was scrimmaging against.

I followed Sporty's success as a coach, and I can say that I think his success was due largely to the fact that he talked the language. He told it like it was. His kids believed in him and he did a tremendous job.

Sporty had a nickname for everyone. My name to Sporty was Mutt. We had a big old boy who was tough as a boot who was named James Cornelius, Sporty hung Corny on him. He had them picked.

We were in school with Harold Tilley, Jack Robey, Vernon Hutchins, lots of coaches in that group. I started out coaching. I coached three years at Texarkana and then I moved to Lake Village and was there for thirty-two years, the last twenty-one as superintendent.

You know Sportys' Daddy was a horse trader and he might start out in the morning with two cows and a calf and he might end up in the afternoon with thirty head of goats, but he knew in the end where he had a market for his animals. Sporty was raised up in that environment, and it made him mentally and physically tough.

Daniel "Cricket" Hunter

Football player

I'm an Arkadelphia native and have always been around the Henderson campus. I became aware of Coach Carpenter when I started to play pee wee football. We played at Old Haygood Stadium. We played on Saturday morning and the Reddies always came by to watch the game after their Saturday morning meeting. I remember Joe Smith, in particular. I have vivid memories of Coach Carpenter in his coaching shorts with his knobby knees and his mouth full of chewing tobacco. I don't know if anyone knows this, but even then Coach Carpenter would talk to me, not many words, and just a few words of encouragement. I was so intense and into the game I just blocked out people's voices. He always waited until the game was over to visit with me.

I don't remember Coach Carpenter actually recruiting me. I remember in junior high and senior high that I would get write-ups with my name in them every time my name appeared in any news-paper in the state or city. I guess that was a form of recruitment because I got little notes and announcements with my name in them throughout my junior and senior high years. The last one I got in high school was concerning the decathlon, the last athletic event of my high school experience. At the same time I did have a lot of cor-respondence with Coach Benson over at Ouachita. The first time I ever really talked to Coach Carpenter about coming to Henderson was the day that I signed. Mark Sanders and I came over to his office one afternoon and talked with Coach Carpenter at length. Mark left and I stayed longer and Coach said, look, I'm going to call Roy (Roy Green) who was home from the pros, and I want you to go home and tell your mother that you are going to sign with the Reddies. Roy and I went to the Henderson cafeteria and had lunch and then went home and told my mom and dad that I was going to sign with the Reddies and play college football here in my hometown. That was my recruitment. I was already a Reddie. I broke my ankle my senior year in high school. The school I really wanted to attend and probably wasn't prepared to attend was Oklahoma State. I got a lot of correspondence from Oklahoma State. I don't know if I was prepared to go that far away from home. But, I had always been around Henderson. Kyle O'Quinn and I were best friends at the time and I spent a lot of time around the Henderson athletic facilities, the pool, the track, the football field, etc.

Just being around Coach Carpenter, I never called him Sporty, not even outside his presence; he didn't have to say much, his intensity spoke for him. He didn't have a whole lot of words and, of course, I didn't say much either. I listened. I listened to everything people said and I made note of everything people did. I noticed that Coach Carpenter was intense. It wasn't about winning and losing for him all the time. It was about the people he cared about.

He allowed me to do what I did best, he allowed me to run track and be a part of the university as well as a part of the football team. He was very generous. I feel like he let me be more than just a defensive back and a football player. He let me use my talent. He let me grow as an athlete and as a person.

I had few problems during my tenure at Henderson; I was in his office very few times. I do remember that when you did go to his office the time was always cut short by the ringing of the phone; he was constantly in contact with players and people from the past. And, of course, he had a nickname for everyone. He had a lot of connections and put people in positions to gain the most for their opportunities. He got lots of people jobs. That included all levels, from trainer to ball boy. He cared for them all. He sat there with the spit bucket between his legs, with his feet kicked up, and there was no formality. What you saw was what you got.

When you first contacted me about the book I was kind of leery, thinking that I didn't have any funny stories or entertaining memories. As I began to mull it over in my mind I discovered that I have many important memories of Coach Carpenter and that he was very influential in my life and in my career. I am not in the coaching field, of course, but how I deal with people. Coach Carpenter coached me to play for the love of the game; he loved football and wanted his players to do so, also.

My relationship with Coach Carpenter was one of mutual respect. Many people thought he was a man of harsh, rough words. That wasn't so with me and I suspect most of his players, if not all. I needed and we needed those one water break days in the 101° temperature practices and those goals he set to be the best that we could be. He provided that for us. The players, me included, were so concerned with their survival that they failed to realize that the coaches were suffering, also. And you guys met before and after every practice.

I have memories concerning Coach Carpenter after I graduated that changed my perspective on dealing with people. I came home one summer and I bailed someone out of jail, one of my ex-teammates. I got a call from Coach Carpenter. He had me come to his office, I thought, am I in trouble? He said, "Cricket, you have to watch who you associate with. You have to take care of yourself and you just can't help everyone." He knew the person I got out. He knew he was in jail and he was not going to get him out. It was like he knew the guy deserved to serve his time to help him. But he was concerned with my welfare, also. The other time I remember was when some of his former players got together and sponsored a vacation for him and Sabra. That is the only time I ever saw Coach cry. He was a very emotional man. We all got letters and calls from him thanking us.

I am reminded of a particular incident involving Coach Carpenter's emotional side when we lost to Arkansas Tech one year and you guys called a meeting on Sunday night after curfew and Coach Carpenter got up and made a inspirational talk about when he played for the Reddies and how he and his teammates would sandpaper their faces to get the blood flowing before a game. I don't think I slept a wink that night I was so fired up.

Henderson, in my opinion, was the best small college program in the country at that time. The facilities, the coaching staff, the talent, were top notch.

Darren Preston
Brother of Kyle Preston, football player

My only personal dealings with Coach Carpenter were when I was in high school and trying to decide where I was going to college. My brother Kyle was at HSU at the time and I just had a few conversations with Coach Carpenter during that time.

From the standpoint of being a high school senior and being recruited by Henderson and Coach Carpenter and the dealings he had with my brother I recognized him as being a great man. Kyle respected him very much. The thing that sticks in my mind is how good he treated his players and coaches.

David Carpenter
Coach Carpenter's only son

Author's note: I interviewed David on the day before his Junction City Dragons were to play Norphlet, a team they were likely to beat by 40 or so points. He was loose and relaxed, mellow in a sort of way that made for a good atmosphere for my visit with him.

I started the interview off with a question, how is it living with the legend? The following is David's response.

It's great, being a coach also, I travel around the state and there's always someone coming up to me, maybe someone I don't even know, who knew Dad, and they will tell me a story or relate an incident that they were involved with him and it's great fun! I enjoy that because I learn a little more about Dad almost every time I go somewhere. Every time I meet someone who coached with Dad or played football with him, or even folks that I know like to tell those stories. It's hard in a way because lots of folks say, why don't you come back to Henderson and coach, and all those things. Dad wanted to be a college coach, I don't. I like high school football; I have a blast at it. At first I started to try the college level, but Terry got pregnant and you know how that can change your plans. College football is not something I want to do. People say, well, your dad coached on the college level. Well, that was Dad, that's what he wanted, and I don't want that.

Growing up I was always a Reddie. We were always talking about Reddie football and all of that. I still remember the day in Wynne when Dad told us we were going to Henderson to coach. It stuck on me hard. We were packing up our junk and back in the sixties you had those little plastic shields you put in your pocket to keep your pen from leaking on your shirt. Well, I had one that I had picked up when we had gone to see the Razorbacks play and they were giving them out and Dad reached over and took it out of my pocket and threw it into the trash can and said, "You are a Reddie, not a hawg!" That has stuck with me all these years. You know, we moved down there when I was in the fifth grade, sixty-six or sixty-seven, somewhere along in there. It is hard for some folks to understand why I don't like the Razorbacks, but it was because of that statement there. It's not that I don't like them, I do, but it's hard to go against your raisin'! I'm a full-fledged Reddie because of that from x amount of years ago.

The next question was, how was it playing for your dad?

His answer was:

It was tough in a lot of ways, especially my freshman year. I remember we were in that drill where you had us straddle that dummy and five or six guys tried to beat the crap out of you and all that good stuff. And every time it got to be my turn to go I would get up on that dummy and Eddie Fullwood would be counting, one, two, making sure he had an opportunity to get a piece of the coach's son! They would put it on me, testing my mettle.

In the spring semester one day, me, J. B., and Whitner, that crew, I kind of fell in with that bunch (offensive linemen) were sitting around and Whitner told me that during my senior year in high school he and other Reddies would come to the high school game and watch me playing linebacker and he said, "Man, I just couldn't wait to line you up in a drill." I asked, "Why?" and he said, "Because I couldn't wait to break your damn neck!" I said "why" again and Whitner said, "I love your daddy to death but all the crap he put us through deserved pay back!" Whitner then allowed as to how now I was just like the rest of the team, griping about him, but being one of the gang. After the fall semester I was accepted like everyone else, suffering along with them, not getting any special treatment, running the fifty bleachers and sprints and all the drills. After that, the good and bad, folks forgot that I was the coach's son and things went well, I was number 83, just one of the guys.

A while back they filmed the postgame of one of our games and looking at the film I told Terry, "My God!" She said, "What?" I said, "That's Dad!" There are so many things I have carried over from him and all you guys I played for, in things and actions that we do, especially in the coaching part of it. We do the same things that y'all taught us. You know, you and I were talking years ago and I was telling you what we were doing and you said, years ago we called it working your ass off and today they call it plyometrics! All those things I learned from him and y'all still carry over into what we do today.

It took a while for my assistant coaches to get used to the way we do things. Like in the locker room before a game, Dad always insisted that we approach the game in a business-like manner, we are going to do this, we are going to do that. We are not going to get into a yelling contest. It has taken a while for the guys I coach to get used to because they have been used to getting in the dressing room and working up a frenzy, calling them gentlemen and all of that, well, that was the way I was taught and trained. I thought I was treated fairly and I want to do the same for these guys here. All these things come from not just playing for Dad but being raised by him. It is a different sort of atmosphere being raised in a coaching family. You know how it was with your kids, you are home so seldom. I tell folks that I never really got to meet my dad until I went to play for him. I was able to be with him twenty-four/seven, the way you were able to do things back then.

When I was in high school and when I went to talk to him in the office it was a totally different thing from when I went into the office as a player. I learned a lot from the association with Dad and all the other staff members, things that I think are pretty good!

My next question had already been answered, but I asked, "How are you like him and how are you unlike him?" Here is how David answered:

There are so many things that I catch myself doing that are the same because I don't know any better.

The coaching thing, and when I was young, on Sunday mornings I would get up and Dad would take me to the field house and drop me off and he would go down to the office and I would start washing uniforms, cleaning the field house, all those different things. He would come back and get me and we would go home, change clothes, and go to church. When I was in the fifth grade I knew how to take care of the dirty jobs involved with some coaching jobs. I knew how to work on equipment, change face masks, you know, fix shoes, all those little things that most guys my age didn't know. In that way I am like him. I just got in from the field house where I have already put another load of clothes on and was poisoning ants when you arrived. I do little odds and ends things because that is the way he did it. I think you always want to emulate your father if you hold him in high regard, which I do. I knew that he was a worker. He was going to try to work harder that anyone and that's what I have tried to do in that respect.

One of the major differences in he and I is not in the way he treated me when I was growing up, because I have been to every sports banquet you can think of, from high school banquets all the way through hall of fame banquets. That was the way he and I could get together and do things. I don't know how many times I have crawled into the back of one of those old school station wagons and lay down and gone to sleep while y'all drove to see some game or recruit some player. I had a good time being with him and all of you guys who coached up there.

When we moved to Henderson it was so late, we didn't have time to find a house, didn't have the money to buy one, so we moved into Foster Hall, the football dorm. That was one of the best things that ever happened to me! I came into Arkadelphia an extremely sheltered fourth grader and by the end of my fifth-grade year I knew a lot of things lots of guys my age didn't get to know! The Braddock twins, Romine, Tom Hogan, and some of those guys were extremely creative with me. How many guys can say, yes, I got hung upside down by a hangman's noose in a dorm room, beat with coat hangers, sprayed with cologne, and left? Tommy Hart taught me some wild things. You remember theses things all your life! That was something totally different that I couldn't give my kids. To have two hundred to three hundred brothers, football, basketball, track, baseball, etc., is a profound thing for a kid. The guys were great to me. I wandered around the dorm and popped up in different rooms and was accepted. When the Braddocks were inducted into the Henderson State hall of honor they had a picture at the presentation of all the Florida boys on the team at that time, and there my head was stuck right in the middle of the picture!

All three of my kids know how to run a trot line and how to do yoyos. That is the direction I went in, not because what Dad and I did was bad, because it was his job, the things he had to do to keep that thing running, but my situation has allowed me to take this approach.

Question number four, how much football did y'all talk in private? David answered: "None!"

When Dad and I came home we never talked football, we never brought film home. The only time film was brought home is when I picked it up from the old Trailway station and brought it to Dad to get it to you guys that day to study. I can remember sitting in old Haygood field house when I was in the fifth grade running that old 16 millimeter projector and running the play over and over, breaking the film and splicing it back like a pro! The coaches would come in and start their meeting and I would sit in the back and listen and that is when I got to hear football; never at home. Dad never tried to coach me while I was being coached by other coaches. If he mentioned anything concerning how I played it was usually a trivial thing, like why did you take your helmet off when you came off the field? Don't be a show boat!

I remember the days at Wynne, we weren't very good but we always had a victory party. Everyone would come over, the coaches and their wives and they would send me to bed and they would get on that old hi-fi and plug it in and play all those old albums, Brother Dave Gardner, Justin Wilson, Sam Cooke, Otis Redding, the Platters, etc. I could hear all the stories that were told and later after moving to Arkadelphia, the same thing occurred at our house, old friends gathering at our house after games telling old stories. It was hilarious!

I still have all the old jerseys from the schools at which Dad coached.

Being exposed to great men was one of the benefits I received from our experience at Henderson. I remember one incident that happened when I was in high school, my senior year. I was out for track and something occurred that caused one of my teammates to be kicked off the track team for what I construed to be an unfair situation. I promptly quit the team in protest and went straight to my dad's office and there were Coach Wells, Coach Sawyer, and my dad sitting there. I told them the story, all three of them told me what I should do. They all three had the same recommendation and shortly after that I was back on the track team.

Last question, what would you like for people to know about your dad?

He did a good job being Dad. We had a different type of atmosphere in our home but you know I wouldn't trade it for anything! I'd get mad 'cause he wasn't around but to get to be around him I spent lots of time down there where he was, hanging out with all the great people with which he surrounded himself.

David Humphrey

Henderson State University, wide receiver, 1978–81; three-time all-conference honorable mention, four-year letterman, four-year starter

In his own subtle way, Coach Ralph "Sporty" Carpenter was all about developing boys into men.

Sure, he was a great football coach. That is well documented. But what sometimes gets lost among the trophies and championships is how he impacted the lives of the players he coached. He was truly the definition of tough love on the field while also teaching the big picture of life off the field.

When I arrived at Henderson State University in the fall of 1978, Coach Carpenter was already a legend. HSU was pounding teams in the now-defunctAIC. Even in losses, we would physically beat teams so badly that they weren't any good for the following week's game.

One of his favorite words was "men." He addressed the team as men whether he was looking at an eighteen-year-old freshman or a fifth-year senior.

It didn't take long to find out why he used the term so often.

Coach Carpenter's practices and verbiage would probably be outlawed in today's game. He wasn't politically correct. He called it as he saw it and he rewarded effort.

Work ethic was big with Coach Carpenter. If you didn't want to work, you might as well leave. Believe me, there were a lot of foot-lockers being dragged down the fire escape in the middle of the night with players checking out.

He also taught us to trust and take care of your teammates on the field and off the field. If someone was in trouble, lend a helping hand. If your teammate is down, pick him up.

He always said the friendships you build on the team will last you forever. He was right.

I still talk with some of my former teammates such at Lawrence Texada, Dwayne "Peabo" Wilkins, Henry "Boo" Pace, and Robert Cooley. HSU graduates are everywhere.

As for me personally, it was simply knowing that Coach Carpenter cared about me as an individual without having to tell me. I don't know if it was the eye contact, the body language, or eventually the calls to my job out of the blue after I graduated just to ask "what are you doing?"

I still remember George Sparks's touchdown pass coming my way during my freshman year that beat Stephen F. Austin in the final seconds in 1978, the joy of going 7–0 and being ranked No. 1 in the nation for one week in 1981 (I don't think it has ever happened again in football) and also feeling the devastation of missing the play-offs as a senior.

I also remember watching a small man with a strong voice transform a bunch of teenagers with a lot of patches on their high school letter jackets into men.

David "Turf" Overturf
HSU, 1975–1979

Reflections of Coach Sporty Carpenter

I first met Coach Sporty Carpenter in the spring of 1975 when he offered me the opportunity to become a student manager/student athletic trainer for the Reddie football team. I didn't know it at the time that this man would become one of the most influential people in my life. Other than my savior Jesus Christ and my earthly father, Coach Carpenter was one of the three men who greatly influenced my life and career path.

I saw directly how much compassion this man had for HSU and the people that worked and played for him. I have heard many of the funny stories and I still use some of his sayings and terminology that he was famous for. The thing that I most remember is how much he wanted all those around him to succeed.

In 1979, I made the decision to pursue athletic training as a career. At the time professional certified athletic trainers were almost nonexistent in Arkansas. Coach Carpenter encouraged me to pursue my dreams, even to the point of helping me find a school to transfer to, knowing that I would have to leave Henderson. When I tried to procrastinate and told him I would wait and go somewhere after getting my bachelor's degree, he insisted that I start the process immediately in order to achieve the goals I had set for myself. With much reluctance I left Henderson after the fall of 1979 to go to Northeast Louisiana University to start the process of becoming a certified athletic trainer, which I successfully achieved in March of 1982.

Without the encouragement and persistence of Coach Carpenter I would not have achieved this goal at this time. This led me to a successful twenty-two-year career in intercollegiate athletics.

I know that I am not the only one that Coach did this for; he just had that special ability to help those around him to achieve their goals. This ability is why he was not only a successful football coach but a great father figure and mentor to those who came in contact with him. I would also like to thank David Carpenter for sharing his dad with all of us.

Deano Norsworthy

Coach Baker, I don't have a lot of stories, especially since I only played for one year, but I will tell you that even after I lost my eligibility due to my not making my grades, he always checked on me when I walked down the halls, he asked when I was going to be back out on the field and would make some comment about my being from Nashville.

I guess my favorite story was when we were having a team meeting and he was talking about the first weekend of school. He said you need to have a watermelon roast pretty soon. One of the freshmen asked, what is a watermelon roast? Coach Carpenter said that everyone gets a date and a watermelon, goes to the bluff and builds a great big fire, you throw in your watermelon and when it heats up it will explode into a thousand pieces. Then everyone goes out in the woods and gets a piece. One of the true freshman with me who was from Canada said, "Get a piece of what, Coach?" and Coach Carpenter started laughing, looked over at one of the older players, and said, "Help that boy out!"

He was a genuinely good man, as all of you were. No doubt I

stayed in school so long (and graduated) because ya'll all took a genuine interest in all of your guys, whether we were Kenny Fells or some immature kid who flunked out after his first year. I tell people all the time that you can directly trace back who I am today to whom ya'll were to me then.

If you need anything else, don't hesitate to contact me. We are starting up next week, but I have no problem taking a break to talk about the best times of my life.

Dick Carmichael

A personal note relates to my sophomore year. I had blown out a disc lifting weights my freshman spring. Therapy all summer had not fixed it. The Little Rock specialist decides to cut on me. I am laying there post back surgery on a fall Saturday morning, probably feeling sorry for myself. Phone rings. It is Coach Carpenter. Now understand this is game day. I am not a starter. I am out for the season, maybe forever. He doesn't identify himself. He doesn't have to. He just starts talking and asking questions. Pretty quick he gets to his point: "Hoss, ya gotta get outta dat bed and get dat first dump outta the way!" "Yes sir." (Pause) "Coach?" "Yep?" "Could you have come back and played after your surgery?" (He had told me earlier about having the same thing.) "Hell yes!" "Thanks. Y'all get after 'em today, Coach." "Good luck to us all!"

Coach Carpenter's First Discussion in Europe

Going to play in Europe, you remember we stopped in Berlin first. They had us deplaning on to the tarmac. There were buses going every direction. No signs. No one directing. I am right behind Coach Carpenter off the plane. He looks around and spots someone standing in the door to a bus and approaches. His question to the guy goes like "Pardon me, dude, is this the mode by which you wish us to exit the establishment?" The very German attendant responds in guttural German that sounds like "Lixs Nik Probell busheden bruska." Coach Carpenter looks at me and says, "The cat can't communicate."

Coach Carpenter on Fine French Fare

One point most guys on the trip to Europe remember is the lack of food served over there compared to what portions were here. It made you eat about anything you were offered. With our last game in Paris, a nice dinner was arranged and as a part of it we were served a slice of cheese that looked like a slice of pie. It was rank. I was sitting close to Coach Carpenter and watching him when he tried a big fork full of the cheese. Splat. He spits it out. "Damn, that tastes like a bear's fart."

His expressions are a part of what we become and are passed on to the later generations.

My kids have grown up crossing streets or watching for blitzes with "keep your head on a swivel!"

President Lincoln, one of the best communicators this country produced, used analogy and it made his message quickly understood. Coach Carpenter did this in his way; describing a combo block, "Tackle brads him. Tight end comes down and spins him like the latch on an outhouse door!"

We played Arkansas Tech at War Memorial in Little Rock my senior year. Maybe Arkansas had an open date that week and this was to promote the AIC ball game. Coach Carpenter took a few of us to a luncheon with the press in Little Rock. When it becomes Coach Carpenter's turn to speak he says, "AIC football is special. Dick, stand up." At that time on a good day I was probably 5'11", 190 pounds. Then he turns to the Tech players and says, "Paul, stand up." Now Paul was Paul White. In high school Paul had set the state record in the shot throwing 65 feet that still stands today. I was at that meet of champs and he beat me by about 16 feet. Paul was huge. The lights were shaded out on his end of the room when he stood up. Coach Carpenter continued, "Paul is a guard, Dick is a guard. In the AIC it is a lot more about the size of the heart." We blew Tech away that Saturday.

As I remember things, I would be happy to share if you wish. What has really set in over time is my belief that what you guys did as coaches at schools like HSU is carry all the pressure to recruit, train, and win that the Nick Sabans of the world carry but without the money to buy your way out of problems. You had to do it just like the guys that did that played for you. You did it for the love of the game.

This book is long overdue, if I can help, please let me know.

Don Dyer

I came to Henderson in 1963; he came in '67 on Clyde Berry's staff. Of course, we played together and had been good friends during our college days. He had been in the navy and got out and came to Henderson. He played center. When Sporty was at Wynne he had a young man who played basketball. Sporty helped recruit him to go to Henderson. His name was Alvin Futrell. Alvin Futrell was a black athlete and Sporty recognized that Alvin had the attributes to be successful, not only as an athlete, but as a scholar as well. Alvin was a hard worker and he contributed to the team's success, but he also was a tireless worker in recruiting other athletes. I knew if Alvin was helping with a prospect he was in good hands. Alvin is probably the reason many good basketball players came to Henderson.

Sporty and I were good friends; he would come to all basketball games if it was possible. He supported us and we supported him and football. I attended all football games if I was close enough to attend. After games I would go into the dressing room and congratulate his players and he would do the same.

Donny Manning
Baseball player

My relationship with Coach Carpenter was very good. It could not have been any better! I remember the middle of my senior year; I was co-captain on the baseball team, one of the four seniors. The seniors were the leaders of the team. We led laps and warm-ups and all of a sudden I am dead last in all the drills and running. I had no energy. I went to the doctor and he told me I had mononucleosis! After my visit to the doctor I was late for practice and I was sitting in the stands crying like a baby, I am not ashamed to admit it. It was the middle of my senior year and I had been doing well, hitting the ball and all. All of a sudden the doctor had told me to go home and go to bed and to not come back for two weeks! I just felt that I could not do that. In a minute Coach Carpenter came up to where I was and asked, "What's wrong, podner?" As I began to tell him my problem he was just like a father or brother or best friend. He assured me that we could work through this problem. That was on a Monday, that Saturday I went to Arkansas Tech with the team, dressed out, sat on the bench for most of the game. Toward the end of the game, we had a pretty good lead and Coach asked me if I wanted to pinch hit. I said that I did and got up to the plate. The first pitch the guy threw me I hit a double off the left field wall. Man, I just barely made it to second base, no energy at all. Coach immediately called timeout and came running out as hard as he could go to check on me. He was concerned about me.

He was a great coach and just a good friend to everyone.

I went to see him the night before he was to have his liver surgery and visited with him for a little while and I am so very glad that I did that! He was just a good friend. He was just a lot of fun to be around, witty and humorous.

Coach Carpenter was a great head coach. He didn't know a lot about baseball but he knew what it took to win and he saw to it that we had and did those things that allowed us to be successful.

I can't put my finger on the qualities he had but I just wanted to play as hard for him as I could. I wanted to show out for him and do well. He knew how to get the most out of his players regardless of the sport.

I think about those days a lot. Sometimes I wake up after dreaming of playing baseball and thinking of those old boys I played baseball with and where they are today. I guess one of the highlights of my life was my senior year and playing baseball for Coach Carpenter and Henderson State.

Doyle Wallace
Fellow coach, friend

While I was coaching golf for Henderson I had occasion to visit with Sporty and his staff. One day after a fall football practice I was sitting outside the dressing room with Sporty having a chew and telling stories. Sporty's wife, Sabra, had been after Sporty to give up chewing tobacco and he had promised her he would quit. As we were sitting there a car drove slowly up the hill toward the dressing room, which then was adjacent to Carpenter-Haygood Field. As the car drew nearer he recognized it as Sabra's car. He had been spitting into a coke can and it was about half full. He said get rid of your chew and with a quick motion he tossed the can up trying to toss it up on the flat roof of the field house. His aim was a little off and the can did not clear the edge of the roof and came right back down. He reached out and caught it and the contents went all over both of us. He handed me the can and said, "You stay here and clean up; I'll go talk to her."

Eldon Hawley
> Career football coach, Southern Arkansas, Ole Miss, Auburn

I first met Sporty in the early sixties when he was coaching at Wynne. I had coached at Wynne two years and then I went out to Texas Tech to work on my master's. Cliff Garrison actually took my job when I left to go to Texas Tech and when I came back to east Arkansas in the summer that's when I met him, when I went up to Wynne to see Cliff. He was up there as the new coach. We reunited later when I came from out west and landed in North Little Rock and he was an assistant at Henderson. He did some recruiting and we talked about players and I went to Southern State in '71 and by then he was head coach at Henderson.

I know the reason he had the success he had at Henderson and I know why people at Wynne thought he couldn't coach a lick. Cliff Garrison will attest to this, the cupboard was bare at Wynne when Sporty got there. Mostly poor athletes and they didn't have a very good attitude, either. I had coached that bunch and left and they had inherited that bunch I had coached in junior high. Not much talent, although their mammas and daddies thought there was lots of talent there. They were in a tough league with Jonesboro, Helena, Forrest City, and Stuttgart, that was a tough league in those days. By the way, you know, he quit at Wynne and became a principal, junior high and middle school principal in the spring semester of his last year there. His statement was, "I've been here for three years and we are not any better now than we were the first fall, so it is time for me to do something else." And then they hired him at Henderson, and he went down there. To get back to my story, the reason he had success at Henderson is because he worked so hard at football, everyone knows he had no hobbies, so he didn't have anything to do but go to his office. He was always busy recruiting, planning, and organizing. How many college coaches do you know who go to Boys' State, because that was a free week of recruiting. He out-worked people, plus

Henderson was a good job. At that time, in the AIC, Henderson and UCA were the best two jobs. He worked hard at it and that was why he had a lot of success. Sporty was one of those sort of guys, who, like a friend of mine who is gone now, Jake Darby, if Jake and Sporty had gone into entertainment they could have done what Jerry Clower did, they had so much BS all the time they were entertaining. Sporty had a nickname for everyone. I was playing in a four ball tournament in Forrest City I met his old boy who was a principal at Marianna and we got to talking and he said he played football at Henderson and I asked him what Sporty nicknamed him. He rattled off a nickname that I have forgotten, but I knew he had given him one.

He called me "Iron Jaw Hawley" most of the time. One time when I went to Stuttgart to coach with Bill Hoskins, who coached with Sporty at Henderson and was kind of dark skinned, so Sporty called Bill, Boston Blackie and he called me Boston Blackie number two. Then he changed it to Iron Jaw. He nicknamed Ken Stephens the Blond Blizzard. He was quite a character.

Ernie "Ironman" Rhone
   Football player, Miami Dolphin

The memories I have of Coach Carpenter during the four years there are that he treated me fairly, he was an honest man , a man of his word. One of the greatest things that I remember about him is that if you played for him and if you graduated he found you a job. Pretty much all of the young men who played there and graduated from HSU would be helped by Coach Carpenter to get on somewhere doing what they had studied to do. He would call all over Arkansas or all over Texas to find a job for the guys wherever they wanted to go. He knew everybody, he had connections. He could find jobs that the individual getting out of school had no connection.

I remember back when I was being recruited, I visited other schools, Southern Arkansas, Monticello, and Ouachita. When I visited Henderson Coach Carpenter took me in his office and he said in his gruff voice, "Look a here, boy, here is what I'm gonna do for you. All my scholarships are taken but I have one coming open at the spring semester. If you come here and play and last until the spring, you got it!" Sure enough, as you know, I came down there and played and sure enough he lived up to his word. When the scholarship became available that spring he signed me. Out of the other schools I visited Coach Carpenter was the only one who had offered me a scholarship.

I have always appreciated the wisdom Coach Carpenter had in not only seeing talent in me but for the guidance he and the other coaches on the staff provided for me.

When I first arrived at Henderson I was a defensive end but at the very end of my freshman year with maybe one or two games left they stood me up as a linebacker and moved me inside, which was a wise move because that is where I played for the remainder of my college career and also for the entirety of my pro career.

There is as story about how I showed up at Henderson carrying my suitcase with no handle and a rope wrapped around it and that I thought I was at Ouachita. As the story goes, Coach Carpenter reoriented me to the Henderson football dorm and put me in his fold. As good as that story sounds, it is not true!

You know how Coach Carpenter was known for giving everyone nicknames; he gave my nickname, "Ironman." That came about from the scrimmages and board drills that we always did. If I got hurt I didn't show it. I took on all comers on the boards and Coach got to calling me Ironman and it stuck. That name caught on at Henderson and today I see people I went to school with at Henderson and that is still what they call me after almost forty years!

My first couple of years at Henderson, Southern Arkansas beat us. My junior year we put a good whooping on them and that is when Coach Carpenter went over there and jumped on their mule and rode him. I think the mule gave him a big old toss and hurt his wrist but he had promised to ride the mule if we beat them and we did!

Coach Carpenter kept a firm rein on his players; he knew all the professors on campus and checked on his players' grades and attendance weekly.

Players are aware of how a coach treats his people and Coach Carpenter did the little things as well as the large things to take care of his men. People might not remember everything but it means a lot to guys like me to have had the nurture of a man like Coach Carpenter. I was similar to many of the young men of that era in that I came to college with pretty much just the clothes on my back. Coach Carpenter saw to it that I survived. I am grateful to him for the opportunity he gave us to play football, get an education, and to better ourselves through athletics.

Under his tutelage we had a lot of success and a lot of fun. I have fond memories of the four years I attended Henderson, of Coach Carpenter and all the coaches on the staff.

George Lafarge
Football player

Early one season we were starting out and it was reported over in front of Goodloe Hall that one of the school's maintenance men had been shot with a BB gun. He was out raking leaves and first he thought he had been stung by a bee. When he went to the doctor it was discovered that the wound was due to a BB gun. Coach Carpenter came into a team meeting and he said, "It's been brought to my attention that one of the maintenance men has been pestered by a BB gun for the last two or three days and I don't want to call any names, but, Ford and Morgan, y'all need to give me that damn BB gun!"

Greg "Skip" Williams
Football player and track star, 1982–1985

I transferred from Memphis State in 1982, Coach Charles Strong, who was a graduate assistant at Henderson, came to Helena after I became unhappy at Memphis State and he told me Coach Sporty Carpenter wanted me to come to Henderson for a visit. I came down for a visit, although, at the time, I didn't know where Henderson State was located. The first two guys I met were Robert Cooley and Albert "Hooty" Boone. I spent the night in the football dorm and the next day they took me down to meet Coach Carpenter. The first time I met him I knew that I wanted to play for him. I knew that I wanted to play for four years, get a degree and that I wanted to coach as my life's calling. It was the best decision I ever made in my life! I loved Coach Carpenter and playing for him was one of the most rewarding feats of my life. I love the man, I miss him, and he was just like a father to me.

I remember that he came to Helena my freshman year at HSU when I was an all-conference player. We attended a banquet there and Coach announced to the audience that I had made All-AIC as a freshman. I was very proud. After the banquet we went to my home and he sat down with my family and we had a good visit. Many times he would invite me into his home where I would eat dinner with him and his wife. Coach Carpenter had a way of treating everyone the same. He loved us all.

These days you hear a lot about guys wanting to play for this white coach or this black coach but I believe that everyone will agree that Coach Carpenter saw no color, he loved us all equally. We were all just Reddies. He bled Reddie! He was the spirit of the Reddies.

It was the greatest time of my life and when I come back to the campus now there are just so many memories there.

The things that he taught me are a part of who I am. I try to be like him in every way that I can. I have patterned myself after him. He is still with us in spirit.

Gus Malzahn

I played for Coach Carpenter in 1988 and 1989. I walked on at the University of Arkansas for two years and then transferred to Henderson for my last two years of eligibility. Coach Carpenter and Henderson was the only coach or school that actually offered me a scholarship as I was coming out of high school.

The main thing I think about when I think of Coach Carpenter is how much he cared for his players. I had just gotten married to Christy and he was really concerned about helping her, helping us, and seeing that we had what we needed to succeed at Henderson. This concern was as strong with our off the field needs and not just for what I could do for him on the field. This made a large impact on me.

In my coaching career I never had a chance to learn under any-one as far as actual coaching was concerned as I became a head coach my second year to coach. As for what influenced me in coaching, I would put Coach Carpenter at the top of the list. He was an example of what a coach should be. Of course, other high school coaches around the state of Arkansas also influenced me greatly.

Coach Carpenter was kind of a legend when I got to Henderson; everyone knew him and knew about him. It was one of those special deals to be a part of that group and, of course, I caught him at the end of his coaching career. He was one of those guys that had that presence about him that caused you to have an immediate respect for him because of that presence.

I have such great memories and such great respect for Coach Carpenter and I was telling his son David the other day when I visited him down at Junction City about the impact his dad had on me, on my life, and my coaching career. I'm asked a lot of times, who have you patterned your life and coaching style after, and he is the one who comes to mind.

Harold Horton
Opponent, coach, and friend

The first time I met Sporty Carpenter was when I was coaching at Forrest City and we were going to play Wynne where he was the head football coach. I looked up and here came Sporty in the gym where I was and he was coming with his usual entourage of four or five people. He comes up to me and says, "I'm Sporty Carpenter." I said, "Coach, it's nice to meet you." With me being young and him being a little older I listened to him. He said, "Horton, you know what we're playing for tonight, don't you?" I said, "No sir, I don't." He said, "We're playing for last place. If I beat you I'm going to put you in last place, if you beat me, you put me in last place." Well, we go out and play the game and Sporty won, Wynne won. And I remember him shaking hands with me after the game and he said, "Horton, I just put your ass in last place." There were three games remaining in the season, and we at Forrest City won two of our last three and Sporty at Wynne lost all three of his games. So, he ended up in last place. That was my first acquaintance and meeting with Sporty Carpenter.

After I came to the University of Arkansas and he went to Henderson we continued to have a good relationship. When I went to the University of Central Arkansas Sporty was head coach at Henderson State. At that time Henderson and UCA were bitter rivals because it was either Henderson or UCA that would win the conference championship. If it wasn't Henderson it was UCA that would win, I think that was the way it was when Ken Stephens was head coach at UCA. There was a built-in rivalry there already. With me knowing Sporty and Sporty coming to Conway every summer to Boys' State and then to the All Star Camp it was just a competitive situation. Hey, he was competitive! He wanted to beat Horton! I don't think it was as much UCA as it was Horton. My first year at UCA we tied 10 to 10 and thereafter I think Henderson only beat us one time, in 1985 when they had Kenny Fells. Sporty probably had a better team and better athletes, but we went on and shared the championship. The thing I remember about Sporty is how competitive he was, how hard he worked at recruiting, how he prized a good walk-on he got to come to Henderson and that was what coaching was all about. We built a good relationship with each other through competition. We were fierce competitors, at each other's throat, but friends off the field. It was fun. I treasure Sporty Carpenter; I think he was a great influence to the coaching profession. When I hear his name mentioned, when people talk about Sporty Carpenter, my heart smiles! That is what he brought to me, joy. I think we both stood for what was best for the game of football!

Harold Steelman
   Opponent coach and friend

Coach Carpenter, better known as Sporty, was such a caring person but a very colorful person, also. I had the privilege of knowing him for a long period of time. He was a very concerned person about his athletes and the people he was around. I worked with him at Boys' State. We were counselors and, of course, I knew him in the coaching profession.
   I think Sporty brought to the Arkansas Intercollegiate Conference

a new wrinkle to the extent of realizing the ability to utilize the PELL grant to recruit young men to come to Henderson and play football.

I know that the men who played for him had an awful lot of respect for him and do still. I know that over the years he touched many young men's lives in the state of Arkansas. Because of their association with him I know that they feel that they have a better life today because of being with Coach Carpenter.

I don't think that what he did for young men was to get a pat on the back for Sporty Carpenter but to ensure that the young men he had charge of were more able to go on and have a better chance to succeed in life.

There are so many good things you can say about Sporty Carpenter, and I just feel honored and blessed to have had the opportunity to be together with him on the occasions I have mentioned, Boys' State and coaching and such. He is sorely missed by all who knew him.

Harold Tilley
Friend, opponent, coach, and fellow student

I'm not sure when exactly it was that I met Sporty Carpenter. In 1953 I got out of the navy in August and about a week later I was out for football at Henderson. I'm not sure that Sporty played my freshman year. Anyway, when he showed up at Henderson after getting out of the navy himself we made fun of him because he had attended school at Monticello (UAM) as a freshman before going into the navy. He went to UAM probably because he was from nearby Hamburg. He went to UAM his freshman year and was a cheerleader! We kidded him a lot about that. I'm talking about over fifty years ago now. I remember that once Sporty got to Henderson he started playing center on offense and linebacker on defense and

I played defensive end and tight end on offense. You know, Coach Wells ran that single-wing offense with an unbalanced line. On my side of the ball we had me, Sporty, and Dwight Adams. I remember some games when Sporty would get on Dwight, telling him he could give us more help on that side! I remember us playing Austin College and they had a big old running back, about six-three and about two hundred and fifteen pounds, and he ran with his knees pumping, he broke my nose and generally ate our sack lunch on our side of the line. He ended up playing for the San Francisco Forty-niners and he was also a pro scout for many years out of Tulsa, Oklahoma. I can't remember his name but it was our first game of the season. You know, back then you played both ways and Coach Wells only played twelve players in that game. He only substituted one player in that complete game, the other guys didn't get to play. We talked about it after the game and I guess we tried to beat them, but that big running back done us in and we lost about 27–12 or thereabout. At any rate, Sporty and I became real good friends while we were at Henderson but Sporty had lots of friends. He knew everybody and everybody knew him because his name was Sporty. He was always one that was a big storyteller. He loved gathering a crowd and expounding on different subjects. When he wasn't playing football he usually had a chaw of tobacco and was spitting in a cup. His language was, let's just say, colorful. He was a "man's man." He was a guy who could draw a crowd of other guys and tell a story and get a big laugh. He always tried to have a laugh at the end of what he was telling and he just about always got it. That's probably where he started coming up with this "lightning struck the outhouse" kind of thing. That quote came from the game the year before I came to UAM. That was Quntius Crews's era. Two years later Henderson came to Monticello undefeated and number one in the nation again and we beat y'all. That night he told the reporter that we should have stayed home and watched Barbara Mandrel and that got a big laugh. I kidded Sporty a lot after that game, I told him he spent too much time thinking about what his saying was going to be.

I think that during my seven years at UAM I beat Sporty three times and he beat me four times, but we had some great battles. I won the three games at Monticello and he won the four at Arkadelphia. I can remember wanting to threaten to kill him when he called timeout with a few seconds on the clock to score a touchdown when y'all were ahead by 30 points. We met after the game and we discussed the situation.

Sporty was the only coach that I played who would call me during the season just to visit. He would call my house during the week before the game. He called me every week during the season and also most of the year. I told him don't call me the week of the game because I'm not going to tell you anything! Can you imagine the opponent's coach calling you on game week? How y'all doing? He was quite a guy! When I was coaching at Pine Bluff one night, we were playing a tough Hall High coached by C. W. Keople and I'm in a frizzie, running up and down the sidelines in a real tense situation when something kind of bumped me on my right side and I look up and Sporty is right beside me. I said, "What the hell are you doing down here?" He said, "This is a good place to watch the game." I told him if he knew any plays that would work we would run them.

I was at Helena when the headlines on the sports page came out with the news that Sporty Carpenter was dead. I could not believe it. Greg Williams, whom I had just hired to coach with me, brought me the news. Greg had played at Helena and Henderson and was one of Sporty's young men.

Also when I was coaching at Helena, after my stint at UAM, Sporty would always call me wanting me to hire one of his boys. I ended up and hired about three or four of his guys. He always had the best interest of his players at heart.

Larry Perrin
　　Player, mid–1980s

I can't believe I am telling this, but if you remember, I got in trouble my freshman year for being in the girls' dorm after hours. It was innocent but I was there. Coach called me to the office and said, "Rodney Parham," (he called me that for some reason), "I ain't mad that you were on the ninth floor of the girls' dorm at three in the morning. I am mad that you got caught in the girls' dorm at three in the morning." And then he issued the punishment, he said, "Son, you owe me fifty hills, and up and down is one." That meant I had to run the stadium steps.

　　Coach, you probably remember this. It was coming up a storm one day before practice and we were stretching. A large bolt of lightning struck close with a resounding crack of thunder, Coach said, "Rodney Parham, I don't know about you, but I'm getting the hell out of here." And, he took off for the barn. He called the field house the barn.

　　Last one—Coach was reviewing my grades one semester, and he called me in. I had been placed on academic probation for that semester, which started my demise in college. He spit in the can, looked over his glasses, and said, "Son, I believe that you have to be the blankety, blank dumbest, smart guy I have ever met. If these grades don't come up you'll be pumping' gas back in Blytheville before the semester is out." And he ended it with giving me some words of encouragement, "Rodney Parham, yo ass owes me fifty hills, and up and down is one." At that point, I knew he still had faith in me.

I have a million more, but no time to write them down. I loved that old man and would have run through a wall for him. One of the greatest disappointments in my life was letting him down academically. I really do miss him; he is a big part of who I am.

One more—we were scrimmaging one day and Fells called 47 pitch, which was a sweep to my side. I was split wide on that play; normally I played a close slot at z-back. When the play was called, I cracked back on the strong safety. His last name was Iverson from Stuttgart. Well, I clocked him. Before I could get up, Coach was picking me up by my face mask, jerking me around, and yelling, "That was the best damn crack I have ever seen." He scared the hell out of me; I thought I had done something wrong. He was very excitable.

I hope these help.

J. B. Grimes

Football player, 1973–1976; offensive line coach at Kansas University

I played my high school ball over at Clarenden and I was a walk-on at Henderson, I wasn't a recruited guy and as I look back on it now, I wouldn't have recruited me, either!

I will never forget when I visited colleges after my senior year in high school. I visited Central Arkansas, at that time it was Central Arkansas, we went there and watched them practice and I never even talked to a coach. We went over to Ouachita and watched them practice and I never talked to a coach. And we came to Henderson and watched them practice; this was in the spring of 1973. We went in there and watched Henderson practice and the first thing I noticed was that there were a whole lot of really good football players on that team. We were getting ready to leave, me, Ronnie Davidson, and Robert Hester and again, we hadn't talked to anyone because we were just not highly recruited players. We were getting ready to leave and Coach Carpenter was sitting in his office and he said, "Hey, y'all come on in here and sit down." All we had to do was to sit there and listen to the guy and that's where we just knew that we wanted to come to Henderson. He took the personal time to talk to us. Out of that group he got Robert Hester, who became an All-American, and I ended up being a contributor and team player. Thirty-eight years later I am still in football, thanks to the foresight of an unusual man.

After watching Henderson practice that day in 1973, I was convinced that if I came to Henderson I was going to be on a team that would win some football games. As it turned out, we won forty games in the four years I was at Henderson. I played in 1973 as a true freshman and I took my redshirt year in 2009 at Mississippi where I was on full scholarship!

In the spring of 1974 I had worked myself into the position to get some playing time as one of those pulling guards but I was still a walk-on. In the fall of 1974 I learned that I was not going to be on scholarship. Coach Carpenter always called us in and informed us as to whether we would be on scholarship or not and I was told that I was not on the list. When he told me he wasn't going to be able to put me on scholarship it hurt me deeply! I almost gave up the game. I tell people this, I went home and talked to my folks and at the end of the day, and I could not give it up. Other than marrying the woman I married, this was the best decision I ever made, not giving up the game I loved and have been evolved with for so long. Coach Carpenter was instrumental in my decision and in my success in the game of football. I played on that '74 team and at semester of 1974 Coach Carpenter put me on scholarship. I was able to be on scholarship the remainder of my career at Henderson. I think he just liked me because I was not a very good player. I was a try-hard guy. He was a special man and he played a pivotal role in getting me into college football coaching. I was like a ship without a rudder there for a while after I graduated. I coached at Nashville for a while and then at Des Arc and then Coach Carpenter hooked me up with Coach Harold Steeleman down at North East Louisiana. Coach Carpenter got me a graduate assistant's job down there. At North East I got a chance to work for John David Crow, a legend in the game of football.

Coach Carpenter profoundly affected my life and my career of being a ball coach. Many of the things I teach and believe are the things I learned from him. When it is all said and done, being a football coach is about people, relationships, and the lives of young men. Coach Carpenter was well schooled in this art. He was the best at building relationships and sustaining them through loyalty.

Author's note: JB was and is the poster boy for over-achievers! He was small but quick and smart. He was one of Coach Carpenter's dogs, and he has established himself as one of the best offensive line coaches in America.

Jeff Atkinson

Football player, 1984–1988; HSU graduate, D.D.S., 1989

Like many young men who passed through the HSU football program, Coach Sporty Carpenter had a big influence on my life. I feel privileged to be included in this fraternity of men he taught. I remember during his funeral service, Brother Bob Trieschmann, our trainer, who also gave the eulogy, commented that one could write a book with stories, sayings, and feelings about Coach C. I am glad that Coach George Baker has undertaken this endeavor. Although Coach Carpenter was not a man who let himself get real familiar with his players—I never even knew where he lived—we would become very familiar to him. My parents loved him, and he made it a point to always speak to them after a home game. When my grandfather died in 1988, Coach C. called me into his office to break the news. He somehow found out even before my folks told me. Coach Carpenter was a tough coach from the old school of coaching. Practices "seemed" long, water was a luxury, and if you were an offensive lineman, well, you've got your own stories to tell! But deep down he really cared for us and more than anything wanted us to become productive citizens after football. I think that is what he was preparing us for, ultimately. I remember he once told us that after he finished coaching, he wanted to buy an RV and travel the country searching for all of his former players. He was going to thank them and make sure they had turned out OK. That would have been some road trip. Coaches may not realize the impact they have on a young man's life. The things they say and do can shape a person's psyche and make him accomplish things he wouldn't have otherwise. I know the good ones realize this and I know Sporty did, too. I can remember after twenty years, specific, special things he said to me after certain practices and games. I'm forty-two now and as I jog around the high school track, trying to keep the belly fat off, I can still hear him in my head telling me to keep pushing—"Come on Atkinson, your the fastest linebacker out here and in last place!!"

I'm a coach now myself, little league soccer, that is. This past season, when a six-year-old was complaining about his teammates, instinctively I said these words, "Don't worry about the mule, son, just load the wagon." He will understand someday!

Jim Bailey
> Sportswriter who covered the AIC during Coach Carpenter's tenure at Henderson

I attended a meeting of AIC football coaches one year and I was sitting adjacent to Sporty when Rip Powell of Southern State College came into the meeting. Rip was dressed in his blue Mule Rider jacket, his Sunday white shirt and dress pants, and a pair of what Sporty called perforated shoes, about twenty years out of style and looked like he had been milking in them. He greeted everyone and everyone greeted him and Sporty turned to me and said, "That damn Rip don't resemble nobody."

I was in Sporty's office one day and we were talking about nothing in particular when he got a call from an English instructor concerning one of his players. After hanging up Sporty related to me what the call was about. He said, "That kid tries hard, he works very hard; he puts in the time, if he could only make a sentence!"

On a similar visit to Sporty's office in the middle of the week during a season, Sporty was cutting articles from the newspaper supposedly to put on the bulletin board to impassion his players against their next opponent. Sporty was looking at all these articles and he had a small pair of scissors and when he came to a part that did not fit with the impression he was trying to put across to his players he would cut it out. I sat there and watched him do that for about an hour and said, "Sporty, you're not going to fool your players cutting out parts of the articles. They will see in the papers that parts are missing." Sporty never let up; he said, "Those SOBs don't read the newspaper."

Concerning Sporty's propensity to hang a nickname on a player brings to mind a player from the early seventies, Larry Thompson. I never heard Sporty call the kid anything but Monk. I learned later that Larry had been coached in high school by one of Sporty's good friends, Jim Montgomery. Sporty called Jim "Monk," so when Larry came to Henderson, he became Monk. He had method to his madness.

Author's note: Jim Bailey was much more than just a columnist to Sporty; he was a friend and confidant.

Jim Ford
Football player, 1972–1975

It was great to talk with you and find out about this book you are putting together. As one of Coach Carpenter's (out of respect I will never refer to him as Sporty) offensive linemen, I am more than happy to share some of my fondest memories with you. Just to start, I am Jim Ford; not to be confused with John Ford, who was our tight end and a senior when I was a freshman in 1972. I started for Coach Carpenter on the offensive line for four years. Including JV games, I started in fifty-five games for Coach Carpenter. I played on the '72–'75 teams that won three consecutive AIC championships and finished the '74 and '75 seasons as the #2 rated team in the NAIA.

Coach Carpenter was much more than just a coach to me. He was a mentor, an inspiration, and someone who gained my utmost respect from the very first minute that I met him. The offensive linemen had the good fortune of having Coach Carpenter as our "position" coach. He loved coaching the offensive line. He loved the physical contact of the drills on the "boards." He really enjoyed the man-to-man battle that took place on those boards. We really enjoyed playing for Coach Carpenter. The other players were not subjected to the "sayings and quips" that we got on a daily basis. I am going to share with you some of these and I will do my best to spell them out in the vernacular in which he said them.

Everyone (at least all of the offensive linemen) got a nickname from Coach Carpenter. John Ford and I were called Foed—the "r" was dropped in the pronunciation. Joe Yancey was Josephus. Jim Morris was Mow Reese. Larry McAlister was Big Mac. Pat McGuire was Little Mac. Nathan Gills was Nasty Nate (so named because Coach Carpenter did a room inspection in the dorm and Nathan's room was less than clean—his roommate was Danny Goddard so the two of them were named Nasty Nate and Dirty Goddard by Coach Carpenter and the monikers stuck). Almost everyone on the team had a nickname but I can't say for sure if Coach Carpenter named them all or not.

Oftentimes when Coach Carpenter wanted a drill or a play repeated in practice he would say, "Let's do it one mo' time with feeling."

When I moved to offensive guard my sophomore year, Coach Carpenter was telling me to pull out and block the corner back at the corner as I led the tailback on the sweep play. His instructions were, "Foed, cycle [he pronounced it sickle] out there and BLAP, knock that corner on his ass."

During a drill one practice, he admonished one of the offensive lineman by saying, "Good golly, boy; you look like Tarzan but play like Jane."

Once, when talking about a road game, Coach Carpenter talked to about us staying at the Rah Mah Dah. It took me a while to realize that he was talking about a Ramada Inn motel.

Coach Carpenter oftentimes would call one of us "hoss fly" or "buddy ruff." I'm not sure exactly what this meant but he said it a lot. Sometimes during practice he would tell the offensive linemen to "grab a root and growl."

Coach Carpenter called his offensive linemen his "dawgs." I don't know if he continued that practice later on but between '72 and '76 we were dawgs. We were proud to be his dawgs. The downside to that was sometimes the dawgs got a little extra practice time pushing the sleds after the rest of the team had already gone to the locker room.

I was always amazed at his being able to chew his Beechnut chewing tobacco and spit into the neck of a 6 oz. Coke bottle while sitting in a chair. I thought it amazing that he never missed. Usually he did this during the hour or hour and a half before kickoff on game day. He was very intense at this time and very little conversation was taking place. He wanted everyone quiet, resting, and totally focused.

Coach Carpenter was a very emotional coach. I really liked that about him. He was not afraid to show emotions when happy, unhappy, mad, etc. In 1973, we beat SSU at home and it was a very emotional win for Coach Carpenter. We, the players, knew that there was no love lost between Coach Carpenter and the SSU coach, Rip Powell. After the win, Coach Carpenter jumped up on the back of their mascot, a mule. He got bucked off but it was great to see him do it!

I will always be grateful that Coach Carpenter gave me the opportunity to play and attend Henderson State University. This is just what this "Okie" needed in 1972. I made lifelong friends, received a good education that has served me well in my professional life, and have fond memories of a great four years playing on a very successful football team.

I hope this information helps you with your book on this outstanding man.

Jimmy Jones
Friend and colleague

There are several things I would like to share about my friend Sporty Carpenter. I have a list in my mind of his strong suits. I don't know if there is a first, second, or third but just let me go down the list of several things that I really enjoyed about Sporty. One of the things I enjoyed in working with him over all those years was that he worked closely with the academic community and he worked hard to get his players educated. That always impressed me, we did a lot of work together and also, we did a lot of follow-ups in getting kids jobs. I knew what the kids would be able to teach and Sporty knew what they would be able to coach. We sent a lot of young men out into Arkansas and especially into east Texas.

Another thing I liked about Sporty was that he would hire good coaches and let the coaches coach! He knew what his strengths were, and he knew what his weaknesses were and there is a lot to be said for that. He did not try to micromanage. He gave you a job and he let you do it. That was very impressive to me, not many people can do that. So many coaches try to do it all and I have always said that one monkey won't make a circus!

Sporty grew up kind of "Sporty" and he knew how to handle kids. He knew how to keep kids within the program. A lot of times kids would mess up and he knew what type of discipline needed to be administered. As I remember Coach Baker did most of the getting up early to apply whatever means Sporty chose to get the job done.

Sporty did something that is not being done today. He worked extremely hard to keep his kids in school and to ensure that they had an opportunity to graduate. It would be very interesting to see the graduation rate of athletes who participated during Sporty's tenure; it was very high. It would be hard to match his record I know.

I enjoyed some social life with Sporty; we discussed things just about every day. I'd go by and visit and we would cuss and discuss what needed to be done academically or in job hunting. As you know, Sporty stayed on the phone all the time staying in contact with the kids. He never got through with kids. When kids graduated he stayed in contact with them.

There are just so many things that don't meet the eye concerning Sporty's stay at Henderson. People look at his record but his ability to work with people was as much responsible for his success as was his ability to coach football. I could go on and on but I am more interested in giving him the accolades he deserves than I am in telling the stories.

Sporty was a Road scholar, not a Rhodes Scholar, he knew people and he loved people. They, in turn, loved him.

Joe "Rerun" Gallop
Manager and friend

I first met Coach Carpenter at Boys' State on the campus at UCA. That was in the summer of 1977. I bought a UCA t-shirt at the bookstore and Coach Carpenter sent me a Henderson shirt the next week in the mail. That is when he asked me to come to school there. It was a great deal and a great time. He never treated me like just another equipment manager. He expected a lot more out of me than that. I called recruits several nights a week while the laundry was being done. I did the official stats. I even voted for him in the national NAIA polls a few times. I have often wished that when I left Henderson that I had come to him to get help. My dad just crushed me and I wanted to get away. I joined the army and that closed the book on that chapter of my life.

Coach Carpenter was a very colorful man. He wasn't the kind of guy that was touchy feely. If you were around him enough you would get a glimpse of him personally but it was rare. I drove him to speaking engagements and he would talk to me some then. He was a very superstitious man as well. His pregame rituals were surreal. He would take the water hose and spray down the sidewalk next to the field house on Friday afternoon. Then he would have me get out the Black Magic shoe polish so the guys could polish their shoes before the game. One day he told me about serving in the navy during the Korean War. Out of the blue he was telling me about having to go to general quarters during an air attack. That was it. We never talked about it again.

Coach was unique in that he had a very tough exterior covering up a very big heart. I saw evidence of that often. I made a lot of embarrassing mistakes as a young man but he never remembered them. He never held anything against me. He trusted me. He once sent me to El Dorado to help Albert Boone find his personal belongings after his mother abandoned them. Albert was a tough linebacker from an even tougher background. It was a very tough day. Coach just handled it and no one ever knew. He was a class act. I was very fortunate to get to know Coach Carpenter. I have had a lot of tough days but I was prepared to handle them because he made sure of it.

I miss all of my Reddie teammates. I miss you, Coach Baker. I do think of you often. I enjoyed the preview of your book on blurb.com. Thank you for the pictures you sent. I especially thank you for writing this special book about Coach Carpenter and for taking the time to call me. God bless you and your family! I'll talk to you later.

Joe Smith
> Football player, track star

I first met Coach Carpenter back in 1973. It was at the Arkansas High School Football All Star Game. Coach Carpenter was not only my head coach, he was also like a daddy to me. Coach Carpenter treated me that way; he treated all his players that way. I felt that he had a special interest in me. I felt like I could go to him for anything. He had a little old short line for everything but the bottom line was that he was for you. He made me feel just like David, his son. I knew that he loved me and not just as a football player.

I remember the first time Coach called for a running back to come into the scrimmage in practice and I ran in there. He asked me, "Who sent you in, boy?" I said, "You asked for a running back, Coach. You didn't call a name." He said, "All right, let's see what you can do," and he called "28 toss." I didn't know the play and he let the defense know what we were going to run. The first time I laid my hand on the ball in college I went eighty yards for a touchdown. After practice Coach Carpenter came by my locker and said, "I don't know your name and I don't know where you came from but I do know you ain't leaving here!"

He treated my wife, Gloria, the same way he treated me. Gloria and I have talked about him many times, he was just so caring for us. He always told me that anyone who came from Gurdon was a good person, to always treat her right, because I know she can cook!

I coach like him and like the way you guys coached me. I have been in the same job for thirty-two years now and I still do things the way he did things because I believe it is a good way to do. When I played ball I enjoyed what I did and I try to pass that feeling on to my players.

If it wasn't for Coach Carpenter I would have never accomplished what I accomplished.

Many times I would go to his office and talk about situations, not just football but about my life and family situations and such. He would give me some of those one-liners he used and we would hash it out.

Everyone had a nickname. He called me Josephus!

I didn't drop the ball many times but one time my sophomore year I fumbled the ball and when I came off the field he looked at me, spit, and said, "Boy, that's the first time you have dropped the ball since you have been in camp." I said, "Yes sir, but I won't do it again." He looked at me and said, "You know damn well you won't because if you do I'm sending you back to Florida!"

I'll never forget one year he called me to his office to tell me he had some more guys coming up from Florida. He said he had a nose guard who could run as fast as me and was much larger. Sure enough he had Eddie Fullwood. Eddie was a nose guard who was also a member of the HSU track team for four years. After Eddie came, when we scrimmaged the defense I would tell Jimmy Morris, our center, to hold Fullwood so I could run the ball without Fullwood hanging around my neck!

I will never forget one day we were scrimmaging and I looked over on defense and y'all had Lyn Young, Eddie Fullwood, Johnnie Gross, Wilbert Hunter, and Ernie Rhone on defense. Coach Carpenter told me to just get as many yards as I could, he knew we had a strong defense. I said, "Coach, I will try but we are going against the best defense in the nation."

Coach Carpenter was not only my coach and like a daddy to me, he taught me football and he taught me life. He told me that what a man would do on the football field he will do in life, if you quit out here on the field you will quit in life. It gets tough out there on the field and it gets tough in life, in your marriage, in your job but if you continue to fight you will prevail. I believe if you believe this and if you believe in God everything will work out.

John W. "Doc" Crawford
Professor emeritus of English Language and Literature, Henderson State University

Sporty Carpenter was a colleague and a friend. After I became director of freshman English and later chair of the English department, Sporty and I worked together well.

Sporty knew that I was concerned about all students' reading and writing problems. When Henderson State secured federal funding for remedial studies, I was designated director of freshman English.

The federal funding included money to establish a full-time remedial reading program, including hiring a full-time reading director. Norma Bryant was hired for that position, so Norma and I worked hard to establish a coordinated program of reading and writing. As head football coach, Sporty realized the importance of having his players succeed academically, so he in turn supported our efforts.

My faculty in English and Norma's reading faculty did our best to get remedial students ready for the regular writing program. Sporty was wise in knowing that he needed good players who would remain in college, and with good reading/writing skills they had a better chance of passing other academic courses, including those in the physical education department. In later years Sporty continued to check with me on a monthly basis about particular players he was concerned about. He never made demands or excuses—he simply wanted to know where those players stood.

Later on I served on a committee that oversaw the use of the Wells Center for Physical Education and there I got to know Sporty even better as an out-of-the-classroom person. He was a fun person, frequently joking. He knew that I enjoyed sports, seeing me at both basketball and football games a lot, but he also knew that I was no expert on the technical aspects of sports. However, he never talked to me in a condescending manner. He did not mince words, but neither do I when the matter is serious, so I understood where he was "coming from."

Sporty understood the importance of school spirit, and that the Greek community at Henderson State provided the bulk of it, so he encouraged my work with Phi Sigma Kappa and other Greek groups. The day of Sporty's unsuccessful surgery, Phi Sigs was hosting a winter conclave at the old Caddo Valley Holiday Inn, where Sporty and his coaching staff and I had eaten lunch many times. When the news came that afternoon that he had not made it, some of my Phi Sigs grieved with me, for they respected him, too, for his hard work and success as coach. Henderson State lost not only a hard worker, but a lot of spirit in the sports arena. That spirit has not been recaptured since his departure. It was my pleasure and honor to know Sporty Carpenter. As long as my memory holds, I will remember

Sporty and his contributions to the sporting world of Henderson State.

John "Kitch" Kitchens
Football player, Class of 1980

Coach Baker,

Sorry for the delayed response. I had a few unexpected things come up and didn't get this together as soon as I had hoped.

I actually have two girls and a son. My oldest daughter is studying to become a physician's assistant and her sister is in journalism school at the University of Florida. My son is starting at UF this summer in the engineering school. Both girls are 5'10" but can you believe that my 17-year-old son is 6'7". He played basketball but went from too big to play weight-class football to too skinny to play in high school.

So here are my top three most memorable Coach Carpenter moments:

Blisters on top of blisters. Any old dog (dog as in offensive lineman) who played for Sporty in the years where the ROTC monkey bars were adjacent to the practice field will remember the pain inflicted by those bars on their hands and fingers. Most of us couldn't hang on the bars without pads when we first arrived for freshman practice. Imagine 250 lb. plus dudes, plus the weight of their equipment, having to race across monkey bars about three times the length of what you would normally find. Then to develop blisters . . . and blisters under those blisters . . . on our hands and fingers that would get ripped opened every time we got on the bars again. Most of us would fall off after only one or two bars. I honestly didn't think it was possible to go the whole way through. But before we knew it, all of us would get through . . . one bar at a time, two bars at a time, and even backwards. This was just one of the many ways Coach showed us how to push beyond the pain and deliver more than we even knew we were capable of achieving.

"Dancing with that boy." In an early game in my freshman year, I got hooked up with a defensive lineman, stood him up and maintained contact for a good while. We were watching films as a team and Coach Carpenter embarrassed me by saying, "Look at ole Kitch; he's dancin with that boy." I wasn't sure at the time if his comment was positive or negative . . . but learned later on that it was a good thing, it's funny how that experience has stuck with me for more than thirty years.

Chicken neck award. In my first starting game as a sophomore, I think we played at East Central Oklahoma, and it was hot, hot, and hot. I hadn't rested well the night before and the players in my room, whom I won't name, ate a bunch of junk food that we shouldn't have. Anyway, it was scorching hot and I played an awful game and felt miserable the whole way back to campus. When I came to the locker room the next day, Sporty had placed some nasty chicken neck bones on my locker and informed me that I had earned the "Chicken Neck" award for my game play. Just what a guy needs when he is feeling bad . . . but I'll tell you, I don't think I ever received that prestigious award again the rest of my time playing at Henderson.

<#>

Coach Baker, let me know if this will work or if you need anything else.

John Launius
Opponent, Southern Arkansas quarterback

Coach Baker,
What an awesome thing you are doing!! I am sure the book will be a hit!!

As for my memories of Coach Carpenter, first of all, I grew up in a town of head coaching legends in Coach Carpenter, Coach Benson, and Coach Outlaw. Hell, I was destined to coach!! Each had their own unique qualities and Coach Carpenter was definitely unique. I remember Coach Carpenter sending me articles throughout the recruiting process and the kind hello's as we passed in the community.

Overall, I remember Coach as a tough, old school, ball coach. The day I went to meet him on my official visit . . . I walked in to his office, he leaned over and spit his chew into a can . . . looked back at me and said, "Well, Launius . . . do we got ya??" Which I thought was definitely unique . . . but to the point! I know that I am a better coach now having known a legend like Sporty Carpenter. I hope this information helps.

Johnny Gross
Football player, 1972–1975

Coach, first of all it's good to hear from you and I hope all is going well for you. Our years during this time are my most fond memories and you are a big part of them, thanks. Sorry it took me a while to respond, I am sure you already have many good stories and probably already have some of these.

Late one Saturday night after a long road trip the old Reddie bus broke down on I-30 about twenty miles from Arkadelphia and Sporty was flagging down traffic to get us back (before cell phones). The first to pull over was an 18-wheeler, Sporty asks, "Are you loaded?" I believe if that guy was empty he would have put us in the back of that truck.

At the end of a long hard practice Sporty decided he wanted goal line offense vs. goal line defense (Sporty was mostly an offensive coach and our defense was nationally ranked.) 1st & goal @ the 10.

After the defense holds a couple 2 or 3 times, Coach Mills says if they don't score you'll be here after dark. During the next series the offense scores, you could see Sporty's face glow red and he kicked the ball to the other end of the field. NOBODY GIVES US NOTHING, needless to say we were there after dark.

The first day back after spring break, Sporty wanted to see who is in shape for spring practice. After a hard practice we were running tours (around the top of the bowl and up and down the bleachers a couple of times and around the bowl to the other side and around the stadium). After a couple of laps I was at least a half a lap behind the next to last guy. Sporty gets on the intercom and says, "Come on, Gross, light up one of them Kools and keep on going, boy."

I am sure I can come up with a couple more, but I thought I would send these for now. Of course, my memory gets a little fuzzy sometimes. For instance, not real sure if the goal line story if that was you or Coach Mills.

Keith Bryan
Football player; president, Powell Products, Inc.

My memories of Coach Ralph "Sporty" Carpenter.
I first met Coach Carpenter in the summer of 1983. I came down on a bus from Illinois where I played junior college football. I was coming down to meet him and to display my abilities as a place kicker and try and make the team at Henderson State University.

When I arrived I met Coach Carpenter and Coach George Baker. After we went through the introductions and all I was to get out on the field and basically try out for the team as a kicker. I kicked the ball around the field, did kick off, field goals, etc. What I remember most about that day was Coach Carpenter and Coach Baker told me to kick a field goal but they were going to stand 5 yards right in front of me to see if I could get the lift needed to get the ball over the line.

When they did that I was terrified that I was going to drill one of them with the ball. It all worked out and it actually gave me more of a boost and I ended up kicking really well and the feeling was a mutual one of getting things worked out so I could come to HSU.

Another memory was how I got the nickname "Bozo." Are you kidding me? I had to live with this my entire senior year, but it ended up being a great thing. I was doing kickoff drills one day at practice and I couldn't kick the ball straight. We ended up redoing this drill five times and finally Coach Carpenter got so pissed off at me that he said, "Damn it, Bozo, just kick the ball down the damn field." That was it, the name stuck and that was to be my name for him for the rest of the time I was at HSU. I ended up not minding as I became the person that I always wanted to become, which was a First Team All-American under his guidance and a belief in me that I could accomplish anything. The thing Coach Carpenter could do that was really great was to make you accountable to the team. He had this way about him of instilling in you that each man must do his job for the other man and for the success of the team.

He could also motivate me and instill a belief in me that I was good. In addition to that, I became very self-confident in my ability as the season went on and we ended up winning the league and going to the semi-finals of the national championship. To this day I truly believe that "if Kenny Fells doesn't get hurt, we win the national championship."

Another memory was when we were practicing the week of the regular season UCA game. We were doing field goal drills and I was kicking about a 40-yd field goal. I hit the ball so well that it went over the film crew scaffolding behind the uprights and flew another 30 or 40 yards up into the trees. It was truly one of the best kicks I ever did in my life, the ball just kept going. Coach Carpenter was so amazed he came over with his teeth clenched and walked up to my face mask and smacked me right in the face mask and said, "That's a hell of a kick, son, now do it again." After that, I was so amped up I couldn't even kick the ball straight because I was so jacked up because I had gotten the coach's attention, big time. That week of practice was such a big week, and we were all pumped up because we knew we were going to beat UCA, who hadn't lost a league game in seventeen straight games, or at least we knew we could do it. After that, Coach Carpenter never tried to fire me up like that again because I got too excited and couldn't kick too well with that much energy unfocused.

I also remember that every time we crossed the 50-yard line during a game Coach Carpenter would say, "Bozo, start getting warmed up."

I remember pregame speeches about sacrifice and no fear. His all-time greatest saying before all games just before we left the locker room was, "Men, set your jaw and back your ears, we fixing to go to battle!" Man, that used to fire us all up and get us right mentally.

I remember when I came home late one night past curfew, and he found out about it. He called me into his office and let me know he knew about it and he said to me that "if I ever did it again, he'd run my ass till it dropped off." Needless to say, it never happened again. What he talked to me about after that was senior leadership and what it meant to be a leader and to set the right examples. I've got to say that I really truly to this day love that man. He taught me a lot about myself, about leadership, about team and doing things right. I miss him to this day when I think about him; however, the memories of him and that part of my life are great ones. It's pretty wild to think that here I am 44yrs old. I have all of these life experiences and this coach from Arkadelphia, Arkansas, had a positive impact in this California boy's life to this day. Wow, that's amazing. I mean I will always come up with one of his sayings in certain situations and I always end up laughing.

Ken Stephens

Opponent

I interviewed Ken Stephens via telephone in October 2009. Coach Stephens was one of our most-respected rivals. He should, in my opinion, be credited with bringing the University of Central Arkansas to the level of prominence that Harold Horton and Clint Conque enjoyed in the more recent past. Coach Stephens was a fierce competitor, possessed of an innovative offensive mindset that caused one to be very careful to be fully prepared to meet multiple offensive sets accompanied with motion, shifts, trickery, and a fast-paced game plan that was enough to cause defensive coordinators many hours of planning and lost sleep. Ken Stephens was as good at using his personnel as anyone else I ever had to defense. If he had a talented player he would give that individual many more touches than anyone else on the offense. The guy one feared the most on the Bears' offense would be the one you saw coming from every conceivable direction, position, and angle. Conservation of force and utilization of talent seemed to be a natural ability of Ken Stephens, but I suspect it was also finely honed by long hours of film study and hard work on the field. The following is the result of my interview with Coach Stephens.

George, when I first came in the league in 1972, Henderson was probably the king dog in the conference. They were winning more than anybody else, they beat us three or four years in a row. I really didn't like Sporty too much at first. He beat us up so much. So, I started to look at what you all were doing that we were not doing. I know y'all played great defense and had a lot of speed, so we decided that we were going to find a few players who could run a little better. We did that and consequently we were able to do a little better job on defense and we got better.

The thing I remember most about Sporty, more than anything else, is that he was probably the most popular coach, with the other coaches and players, of anyone who ever coached in the Arkansas Intercollegiate Conference. If he was not the best, he was close to the best. Everybody knew him and everybody respected him. It was a real pleasure, having him in the conference all those years. I have really missed him since he has been gone, even though I have not been in the conference. He was one of the stalwarts of the conference during the years I was in it. The ten years I was in the AIC were ten enjoyable years, Sporty and I had our ups and downs, but we ended up being the best of friends, you remember that, George. We were probably the best friends of anyone in the conference by 1982. It was really fun going to Henderson and playing down there.

One story I remember, is my first year, we were down in Arkadelphia and y'all were beating us, I think, 49 to 0, and y'all were down on the goal line with two or three seconds to go and your quarterback called timeout to get another play in, y'all fumbled the ball and didn't score. After the game, I jumped all over Sporty, telling him that wasn't very nice, running up the score, and he said, "Coach, I didn't do that, the quarterback did it!" I remember that very well, we were going south on the football field. That was probably the worst loss in my ten years in the AIC.

Another thing about Sporty besides the fact that everyone knew him and everyone liked him, is the fact that he had a nickname for everyone. All his players and all the coaches in the league had a special name. He was a colorful, colorful guy.

Author's note: Coach Carpenter called Coach Stephens the Blonde Blizzard, one of Sporty's more complimentary monikers.

Kyle "Mudcat" Preston
Football player

I enrolled in Henderson State University in the fall of 1983 to play on the Reddie baseball team. Halfway through the fall semester I realized how much I missed football. I went to the Wells Center and asked Coach Carpenter what I needed to do to become a part of the Reddie football team. Coach Carpenter told me what I would have to do and when the spring semester rolled around I joined the Reddie football program as a walk-on prospect.

Needless to say, the next four years were some of the best times of my life, times that I will never forget! There were the good times and some times that weren't so good but the thing you could count on was that Coach Carpenter was always there for you.

The 1984 season was a season in which we didn't win as many games as we would have liked but I got something from Coach that I still use today. We were sitting in the dressing room after Ouachita, our across-the-street, in-town rival had just beaten us 24 to 22 in a grueling, hard-fought battle. Coach said in addressing the team, "Gentlemen, in life it is not important what may happen to you. What's important is how you react to what happens to you." There has never been a more truthful statement!

We had a few more weeks left until the end of the fall semester and then we were gone home for the holidays. I had been home for two or three days when the phone rang one morning about 7:00. A gravely voice on the other end of the line said, "Wake up and pee, the world is on fire!" It was Coach Carpenter and he told me that we had a problem but there was a solution. I had not passed the required twelve hours due to dropping a course late in the fall semester and, as a result, had become ineligible. Coach explained to me that he had enrolled me in a midterm course, and it was imperative that I come back to the campus to attend the class. I thought he had it all worked out so I traveled to Arkadelphia and signed in for the class. There was one major problem; I had no place to stay. When I brought this to Coach Carpenter's attention he told me to come by his office that afternoon and he would show me where I would be bunking. The solution was for me to sneak in to Goodloe Hall after dark and he warned me to not let anyone see me coming in or out!

The 1985 football season is one that will be remembered forever.

Larry "Baby" Ray
Football player

Coach Carpenter did a lot for me. One year, I guess it was in 1974, Patty Campbell broke his leg that year and we really didn't have another fullback. I was the only fullback on the squad. About the second game I separated my shoulder. I had to go Little Rock to the doctor up there and Ricky Ford, the trainer, took me up there.

Anyway, the doctor up there looked at my shoulder and said, "I guess we will set you up to do surgery in the morning." I said, "I don't think so." He said, "Yes, we have to set you up for surgery first thing in the morning, you have a separated shoulder and you are through for the season." I said, "Well, you tell me why I can't play." He said, "You won't be able to stand the pain." I said, "If that is all it is to it, I will let you know something in the morning." Me and old Ford hit the first beer joint we got to and it was about twelve or one o'clock when we got back that night. We parked up there behind the field house and we were both in pretty good shape at the time when we got out of the car. Then we heard somebody say, "Where in the hell have y'all been?" We said, "Coach, we have been up there to Little Rock to the doctor," and about that time he got close enough to smell us and he said, "Good God almighty, y'all are as drunk as a skunk!" He said, "Ford, get yourself to the dorm and, Baby, you come down here to my office." I said, "Oh heck, I'm in trouble!" We went down to his office and he said, "What did that doctor say?" I said, "He said I have a separated shoulder." He said, "Hell, we knew that, what is he gonna do?" I said, "I don't know, he said he was gonna do surgery in the morning." He said, "Do surgery? What did you tell him?" I said, "I told him I had to come back down here and let them know something in the morning." He said, "Hell, that doctor don't know what the hell he is doing." I told coach that I told the doctor that I thought I could stand the pain. Coach said, "I tell you what, you get out there in your head gear and shorts and run through the plays and play on Saturday." That sounded good to me but Coach Cerrato ran me off the first day the team practiced in pads and I showed up in shorts. Coach Carpenter explained it to Coach Cerrato in this way, he said, "Coach, I'm gonna tell you, we are number two in the nation and I ain't never been number two in the nation. That boy is gonna stay and he is gonna play." I ended up playing all that year and there was a little pain but I stood it because I wanted to play for Coach Carpenter and for the team. Coach Carpenter stuck with me and I stuck with him.

He did so much for me! So much, one thing and then another, I can't really name all the help he gave me but it was considerable. I have four children and Coach Carpenter was present for all four births. He always brought them a little Reddie jersey with "Baby" on the back of it.

He had "student assistants," and what that was designed to do was to get you through school when your eligibility was over. That was the type of person he was, a helper!

I remember one time he called me back up there one Friday night to talk to the team and I walked through there and I said, "Gosh, Coach, the biggest guy we had was probably Nate or Joe Yancy and Nate probably only weighed 255. Y'all have some 280s and 300 pound guys!" Coach said, "Yes, but I ain't had to get a soul out of jail since y'all left. If you mention fight around here these guys will run."

He could have turned his back on me several times considering some of the things I did. But he didn't.

He told me one time, I went down there, and he said, "Baby, Buddy Bob called me and he told me he had five boys over there that were going to whoop your butt." I said, "No, they ain't gonna whoop me, I took care of them last night." He said, "What in the hell did you do?" I said, "Well, I went over to OBU and picked up old Raney and took him up in the park, whooped him, and took him back to his dorm."

There are so many stories, one time the week before we played Ouachita, an old boy had a keg of beer, me, J. B., Robert Hester, and Randy knew about it. We came in on time for the curfew but got to talking and reminded each other of all the girls still out where the keg was so we went back out there. By the next morning Coach Carpenter had found out about it. He called the dorm and sent for us. When I got to the Wells Building the rest of the guys were sitting there and they told me, he has kicked us off the team. I said, he ain't going to kick us all off the team, they said, he has already done it! He told us to go clean out our lockers. I said, "Let me go talk to him." I walked in there and said, "Hey, Coach." He said, "Baby, what in the hell did you do last night?" I told him that we went out and drank a few beers and came back to the dorm. I told him that there were a lot of girls out there and I reminded him that he had told us to never bring a girl back to the dorm. That's all we did. I said you have the boys all worked up out there they said you were going to kick us off the team, that you had kicked them off. I said you can't kick them off with out kicking me off. He said, "Well, I might just do that!" I said, "No, Coach, I know you aren't going to kick me off; you have had too many other opportunities to do that." He said, "Well,

I'll tell y'all one thing when this game is over I'm going to run you and run you and run you!" That was my senior year and I knew he wouldn't have the opportunity to run me but he sure got those other guys!

He was really something. I miss him.

> *Author's note:* Larry "Baby" Ray was our poster boy for tough! Look up tough in the dictionary and you might find a picture of Baby. He got the name "Baby" in high school, but it did not describe his demeanor!

Leon Anderson
Opponent

When I came into the AIC I was kind of the young guy around and all the AIC coaches knew me when I played for Tech. I always looked up to them and respected every one of them. Of course, I respected and looked up to some of them more than others. Sporty was such a man. One year Henderson had blocked two punts against the opponent before us and I was determined that they would not block a punt against my team. I was young and inexperienced and decided that putting my offensive linemen on the punt coverage would do the trick. That night Henderson did not block a punt; however, Roy Green returned two for touchdowns. Sporty met me on the field after the game. Henderson had beat us about 37 to 7, he threw his arm around me and said, "Leon, get those fat ass offensive linemen off your punt coverage!"

The thing about that league, the AIC, those coaches, the camaraderie and relationships among us made it so much fun to coach. Knowing everyone made you want to beat them so badly. I know I certainly enjoyed beating Buddy Bob Benson down in Arkadelphia one year with a little veer attack that we had—it was just like taking candy from a baby! There were games where we were the top dog and a lot where we were down in the dumps. The league was made up of a lot of really fine coaches and assistant coaches. I remember all of them. Of course, they used me as a whipping dog most of the time that I was there.

Lewis Pryor
    Football player

Needless to say, the story that sticks out in my mind happened when we were playing Mississippi College down there in 1971, I was playing quarterback and we were running the veer option. I ran the option and the read required me to pitch the ball to the trail back and I did. I turned up the field and looked inside to find someone to block. Well, the pitch back was tackled and the whistle blew and I relaxed. I saw a Mississippi College defensive back coming on a beeline from about five yards away. The play was over so I didn't expect what happened. As I turned back to go to the huddle to call the next play he grabbed me by the face mask and all I saw was his fist coming. There is no reason for this to happen. He knocked me colder than a wedge. When I came to, Coach Carpenter was sitting on my chest and stuffing an am cap up my nose. "Louie, come to, boy, wake up, boy," he said and then he yelled, "Get that SOB off the field!"

He was a special man, I was fortunate to play for him and I will tell anyone that. He allowed me a second chance.

Mary Jane Attwood
    Student secretary and friend

Networking was probably invented by Coach Carpenter—R. L. Carpenter was the best ever at keeping up with the "Reddies" and anyone else that could help recruit players as well as students to

Henderson. I was fortunate enough to work for the athletic department at Henderson from 1969 to 1972 and most of that work was networking. From 1973 until he died I think he still considered me to be on his staff as he asked me to "get in touch with," "go by and see," "get me their phone and address," or just "find out about" many people in Arkansas and throughout the United States.

There was not a week or weekend while at Henderson that we did not cut clippings from newspapers, make phone calls, type letters, write personal notes, take recruits on tours of the campus, get Caddo meal tickets, schedule dorm rooms, attend pep rallies, and even talk to the parents of recruits about the "Reddies." If Sporty had had a laminating machine in those days I am sure he would have worn it out or melted it. His philosophy was "the more we talk to, the more we can get to Henderson."

He also felt that all those on campus from my sorority sisters, friends, faculty, alumni, staff, and players of all sports should help with making Henderson the best place to be. Many times for track meets, baseball games, or football, he asked me to get volunteers from the dorm or campus to help. And he had nicknames for them just as he did for those players.

Personally, he was always there for me in the times of my life when I needed advice in my personal life as well as help in dealing with a death of a parent or even job-related decisions. I am sure he was that way with the players, as I remember him helping many with their first job as a coach, teacher, or other employment. He was always on the phone with one of them about their family, work, or sports. When I went to work at the *Arkansas Gazette,* he thought that was just another chance for me to help with more networking. Those days also made me a little tougher and better able to handle most any situation. As I started my career in sales, the things I learned from Sporty have been the most valuable and have been far more important than the sales trainings I have endured. For his training I will always be grateful.

His love for Henderson and the Reddies was an inspiration to us all. When I visited him in Little Rock, that last week he was in the hospital, I mentioned that there was a basketball game on TV we might watch. I think it was Arkansas vs. Texas and his comment to me was, "If it ain't the Reddies, I ain't interested." That was exactly how he felt and it was a great example for us all. He loved Henderson with all his heart. Hardly a day and certainly not a week passes that I don't think of him and treasure what he taught me.

Author's note: In what Sporty called his repertoire of special people Mary Jane ranked very highly.

Mike Bass

Football player, 1982–1984; All-American 1984; Academic and NAIA Football All-American; All-region, Duke Wells award winner

The way I got to Henderson happened like this: I received a phone call in the spring of 1981 from David Lee, a good friend and teammate of mine. His dad had gone to school at Henderson with Coach Carpenter and had known him for years and David asked me if I would be interested in going to visit Henderson with him. I said that I would and later that week I got a phone call and this was before cell phones and caller ID, and this gravelly voice asked if Mike Bass was there. I said, this is him, and the voice said, "This is R. L. Carpenter calling from Henderson State University." He said, "I hear you want to play some college football." I told him, "Yes, sir, I would." He said, "Do you know where Henderson is?" I said, "Yes sir, it is located in east Texas." He said, "Hell no, boy, we ain't no juco, we are a major, four-year university!" That was when I first met Coach Carpenter.

I tell everyone that the four years of my life spent at Henderson State University, being taught, coached, and mentored by Coach Carpenter and his staff, are four of the greatest years of my life when it comes to building a foundation for the success I have had as a coach, an athletic director, a father, and as a man.

His demeanor, his personality and the folksy, father-like way he communicated with us lingers on with me and always will. I loved his use of the language, and still chuckle when I think of his nicknames for me and the rest of my teammates.

One hot fall practice we were trying to survive a two-a-day practice and Donnie Willis had worn a pair of torn shorts to practice, leaving part of his anatomy exposed. We heard Coach Carpenter say, "Willis, I'm looking straight up your gun barrel and it sho is rusty." Fatigue gave way to hilarity and for the rest of the practice, pain was relieved by mirth. What a guy!

Coach Carpenter was far ahead of his time with his use of the so-called monkey bars. We thought of them as torture devices, but were required to negotiate them each practice. One fall someone burned them to the ground. Shortly thereafter, a new, all-steel edition appeared and back to the torture. I heard Coach Carpenter mumble, "Let them burn these down!"

The way I got to be a graduate assistant at Texas A & M is by Coach Carpenter, he called me one day and asked me, in his typical gravelly voice, "Boy, I hear you want to go to Texas A & M?" I told him I did and he told me he had me an interview with Coach Paul, Cash, and Register, who had played with Coach Carpenter at Henderson. Coach Carpenter told me that Coach Register was the defensive line coach and he told me to not mess up the interview, because he had "sold me good!"

I interviewed with Coach Register and he in turn recommended me to Coach Jackie Sherrill. When I got down to A & M

I was supposed to interview that day with Coach Sherrill but when I showed up for the interview they told me Coach Sherrill was in Pennsylvania recruiting and would not be back until the next day …When I found out Coach Sherrill was not there my feathers fell and I decided to just forget my dream of coaching at A & M, where my dad had played ball and graduated and just go back to Arkansas and get me a coaching job and forget the whole thing. So, I threw my coat and tie and shirt over in the corner of the motel room. I had brought only one tie, one white shirt, and a pair of dress pants and about two hours later I got a phone call telling me that Coach Sherrill had just got in from his trip and would be able to see me that day, in about an hour. My clothes were hopelessly wrinkled and so I jumped in my car and rushed down to the local J. C. Penney and bought me a new shirt, pants, and tie and made it to the interview looking sharp. I walk into Coach Sherrill's office and it is dark and he is sitting behind his desk with his glasses sitting down on his nose and he said, "Boy, if you are loyal to Texas A & M and if you are loyal to Jackie Sherrill you can coach anywhere in the United States, but if you are ever disloyal to Texas A & M or disloyal to Jackie Sherrill, you won't coach anywhere in the world. Do you want the job?" I said, "Yes sir!" The rest is history! I got there because of Coach Carpenter. Everybody knew Coach Carpenter and he knew everybody. Everyone respected him.

Another funny thing about my stay at A & M is that when I was there, GA's were unlimited. During meetings the hired staff sat at a large table and GA's sat in chairs against the wall. There were so many GA's that when one guy stood up, two more had to stand up to unwedge him! We had twenty-four or twenty-five GA's and twenty-four or twenty-five student assistants, a thundering herd of men scrambling to do what they could to help the effort.

Mike Dugan

Sports information director and friend

Sporty Carpenter

Without any question, Ralph "Sporty" Carpenter was and has remained one in a handful of people who have had a significant impact on my life. It would be years before I understood some of that impact.

As time has gone by I often think back to something he said or did and like many, many others that were around him a big smile comes across my face. The ten years I spent working for and with him was always a joy. That is a significant statement since the pay was deplorable and the hours at times were worse than the pay.

I always tried to spend a few minutes each morning in his office to find out what was happening with the team, the opponents, or recruiting. He was always totally honest and most stories came with more than a bit of humor. Everyone has their own "Sporty" stories and they all remember his colorful use of the English language. He seemed to always refer to the team as his "mens." Everyone had a nickname. I proudly wore the tag "SID Man." My good friend and across the ravine Tiger Rex Nelson was simply known as "Rexall."

Perhaps my favorite nickname of all time was our basketball manager Jay Freeman from Mammoth Springs. Jay always wore his high school letter jacket that had a stylized Bears written across the back. Sporty quickly noted that it looked more like Beans than Bears so Jay became "Beans" and it never went away.

We had a place kicker from California by the name of Keith Bryan. Sporty was always leaning close to me or an assistant coach to ask the question: "Is it Keith Bryan or Bryan Keith?" To solve this problem the kicker just simply became "Bozo."

One of the wonderful moments I enjoyed with Sporty was a basketball trip to Monticello. A notice had just been sent out by the university that at no time should a state-owned vehicle be seen at a location other than what was listed as an authorized destination. As soon as I picked him up that afternoon he told me to drive to Walmart. I protested but he insisted so I began a nervous wait while he went inside. When he came out he threw his package into the back of the car and away we went.

As we neared Monticello he began to give me alternate directions and sent me down an isolated highway and through the gates of a cemetery. We left the car and Sporty got down on one knee to clean the weeds from his parents' graves, the package contained flowers. This was a wonderful, warm side to a man that I already knew had a big heart.

On another trip to Monticello I told Sporty on the way down that the women's basketball coach at UAM was going to be mad at me that night. At that time I was the NAIA District 17 coordinator, which meant I had to spend several hours each Sunday afternoon gathering statistics to report for the weekly national reports. That week I had left off a UAM player that would have been ranked around twentieth in the nation in rebounding. Sure enough in the hallway between the women's and men's games the coach yelled at me for the omission. As he walked away Sporty said, "Hell, Alvy, Dugan told me he did it on purpose." Well, all hell broke loose then; several people had to separate the coach and me. All the while Sporty was leaning on the wall laughing his butt off!

Another favorite was the time he called me on a Friday afternoon and told me to meet him at Lakeside High School in Hot Springs for their game that night. I asked him why we were going to Lakeside. He responded, "I promised that ole boy up there that I would take a look at a linebacker, he probably can't play but I promised him." That night Ashdown scored on their first four or five possessions to take a huge lead. It did not take long for the parents sitting around us to start yelling at the coach for being an idiot. At that point

Sporty spit a stream of tobacco down through the bleachers and turned to me, saying, "I don't guess it would help for me to tell them that it was their fault and not his," a quick, accurate assessment with a wonderful twist of humor.

For all the funny stories, I think the real story of Ralph "Sporty" Carpenter is the story of the man that helped countless numbers of students. Not just during their time at Henderson but past those days and far into their adult lives. The stories of his time spent on the telephone are legendary. Often those calls were being made to schools looking for jobs for players after graduation. I would wager that he spent as much time doing that if not more than recruiting. When a former player was having a problem in their life it was often Sporty that they called. That also went for former "SID Men."

It is hard to sum up someone like Sporty in a few words. This has been very difficult to write because of that. For many that did not take the time to know him he might have seemed a bit crude and simple. For those of us who knew him we understood just how intelligent and caring the man was. I know he was very special to me and I think of him and quote him often. Never is there a thought or a quote that is not accompanied by a smile. When you leave something like that behind you it is safe to say you led a very well lived life!

Nathan Gills
Football player

Tribute to Coach Carpenter:
Of all the people who have contributed to any success I may have had in my adult life I can not think of anyone I would have to thank more than Coach Carpenter. He challenged me to become more than I ever thought possible. I guess he saw something that I did not see in myself. He had a gift for knowing when to be tough on a

player and when the player needed a guiding hand. I can relate to both of those.

Early on in my career as a Reddie football player, I didn't know what I was capable of enduring but I found out pretty quick. We were in spring practice and short of "O" linemen. As always it seemed there was an overabundance of backs, receivers, and defensive personnel but only seven or eight O linemen if we were lucky. I was the only one in practice that day that could snap a ball to the quarterback. We were having 3-on-3 drills with running backs. The other two linemen got to swap out after three plays but since I was the only one that could snap the football I got the opportunity to continue. I don't know how many plays we ran but I know I was gasping for air and thinking I was probably going to die. Things weren't going very well for the offense, either. Coach Carpenter yelled out, "Nate, quit feeling sorry for yourself and get in the damn huddle." I think I hated him at that moment and it gave me the incentive to endure that drill. I later realized I probably was feeling sorry for myself and I learned that I wasn't going to die as long as I could still gasp. The lesson in this is that I had never been pushed to that point of exhaustion before and it taught me that when pushed we do not know our capabilities.

On the opposite side was compassion. I remember I managed to find a girlfriend one year and like everyone in love I floated around on a cloud until she broke up with me. A few days later I see her (names left out on purpose) at a party hanging out with what I thought was a good friend. Later that night I went to his room looking for him and probably lucky for both of us he wasn't there, but his light was on and I was sure he was avoiding the ass kicking I was determined to give him. I kicked in the door, and he was not there. Monday morning I received a call and was summoned to Coach Carpenter's office. I just knew my butt was toast. He questioned me about what happened to the door and I told him the truth, except the part about the alcohol. He told me I was going to have to pay for the ———— door and I better damn well never let that happen again and get out and get ready for practice. I never received a bill for the door.

During the season of '75, Channel 4 was coming down to shoot some footage for the evening sports show. Coach Carpenter came to me and told me he was going to make a star out of me. He told me while we are running team offense I want you to jump before the snap of the ball and then I'm going to chew your ass out and then I want you to do it again and I'll chew you out good the second time. This will be on camera for the sports tonight. I did, he did, I did again, and he did again, but only real good the second time. It was on TV that night. They didn't have the language on the air just the facial expressions of Coach Carpenter chewing me out. My mother didn't think I looked like a star.

All the special team groups worked before practice kicking, punting, deep snapping, etc. Coach Carpenter found an old horse barn up behind the practice field and moved in some old car axles and weights for the "O" line to lift while everyone else was doing specialty work. There weren't usually any coaches up there and the upper classmen were relied on to make sure the group was working. One day before practice we were up there working out and after getting through with a set of weights I dropped the bar and turned to the rest of the guys and said, "There is too much work going on around here and not enough play." Everyone just stared through me with a blank stare on their face and I turned around and Coach Carpenter and Coach Stiffler, my high school coach from Gurdon, were standing about ten yards behind me. I turned back around said, "All right, that's enough play, get back to work." Coach Carpenter never said a word, he didn't have to.

My freshman season in '72 we were playing a JV game at HSU. We had a screen left called. I was the lead blocker, I got out front and there was no one outside. As I started to turn up field I saw a line-backer coming from inside. I planted my left knee to turn back; I felt it tear as it buckled. I went down and crawled to the sideline. When you blow out a knee you know it. It wasn't long before the half and when we went into the dressing room Coach Carpenter told me to keep ice on it until after the game—it may just be a strain. Dr. Luck came by and looked at the knee and said he felt like it was torn and told me to get dressed and had the manager bring me some crutches. When the game was over Coach Carpenter came to the dressing room and said, "I told you to keep ice on that knee." I explained that Dr. Luck had told me he thought it was torn and to get dressed. That didn't go over well, and he explained to me lovingly that he was still in charge. So, I asked him what he wanted me to do and he said, "It's too late now, we'll have it looked at tomorrow." I never was sent to the doctor again but the next week Coach called me into his office and said that the knee was probably torn and would have to require surgery. He explained to me that we were down to three offensive tackles on the team (including me) and wanted to know what I thought about just getting the knee treated everyday and watch practice on crutches. Then we would wrap it up real tight and I could dress out for the game in case I was needed. He said I couldn't hurt it any worse since the knee was already torn up and there weren't but a few weeks left and I could have the surgery dur-ing the Christmas break and wouldn't miss any school. I said okay and for the rest of the season that's what I did. I dressed out and stood on the sideline until the Ouachita game. Someone actually went down for a play and he sent me hobbling into the game. I don't remember why but for some reason we didn't run the play and I had to hobble back off the field. By the time Christmas rolled around the swelling had gone down and the knee felt better so I wasn't sent for a follow-up with the doctor.

That spring I was part of a group involved in the intramural softball saga and was kicked off the team so I didn't play the season of '73, which gave my knee a year to regain strength as it turned out. That next spring Coach Carpenter invited me back and I started at left tackle for the next three years by getting the knee taped up and wearing a knee brace. I did re-injure the knee a couple of times after college but I would go have the fluid drained off and I recovered after a couple of weeks. Twenty-five years later I started having a lot of problems and had to have an MRI done. The doctor asked me when I tore up the knee. I told him originally in college playing football. He said that I had torn my ACL. Since it was not repaired it had deteriorated and I didn't have a sign of an ACL. The doctor was amazed at how I had played three more years and made it that long. I told him my coach said it was all right and I believed him.

The week of the Ouachita game during the season of '75 was a huge game week. This was supposed to have been my senior season, but Coach Carpenter wasn't finished with me yet. He called me into his office that week and explained that since I had missed the season of '73 that I had an additional year of eligibility. The only catch was that I could not attend school the spring semester and graduate because of the ten-semester rule. Coach said I could lay out and work, come in and practice during the spring and I would be eligible in the fall. He said don't make a decision now, just think about it and let me know what you think. We lost a heartbreaker that week and I found the next week I had been named All-AIC. I told him after Thanksgiving that I would come back. I tell you this story as a lead into the next. I got to go on the European Tour that summer as a result of that decision.

I started the '76 season as a two-time senior. At the end of two-a-days Coach Carpenter called me into his office and said it was time to get some heads shaved. It was a tradition that all freshmen football players get their head shaved prior to the start of the semester. He told me to get the seniors together and get it done that night.

I called the other seniors together and told them that it was time to shave heads. Two of them were adamant that they did not think it was right to shave the freshmen's heads. (Names purposefully withheld) I told them that Coach Carpenter had told me to get the seniors together and get it done tonight. They said we want to talk to Coach Carpenter first. I told them they could wait and talk to Coach Carpenter but I was doing what I was told. The other seniors and I went ahead with shaving heads. There were a few freshmen opposed to the idea but they all saw the light except one. He came up with a story about some rare hair disease and if his hair were cut it would never grow back. I wasn't buying that story but some others did. I was the one that had to answer to Coach Carpenter for it. "Damn it, Nate, I give you one little job to do and you screw that up." I didn't tell him about the opposition to his request and I don't think my two fellow seniors ever mentioned it to him, either. The guy quit before the season was over and I can't say it disturbed me.

My days of playing football at HSU for Coach Carpenter were some of the best days of my life. I wouldn't trade that experience for anything. The friendships and memories I will always cherish, not only the Reddie coaches and teammates but players and coaches from other schools with whom I have friendships developed over the years.

Owen Smith
Newspaper editor

Newspaper Manager Seeks Sporty's Help

Owen Smith, fresh out of graduate school in Rochester, New York, arrived at the *Arkansas Gazette* on July 1, 1978, to begin his career as a newspaper operations manager. By 1980, he had concluded that he needed help in motivating his department to manage as a team, rather than as individuals.

Without first disclosing his purpose, he asked a colleague, an alumnus of Henderson State, who built the best athletic teams in Arkansas. The answer was immediate: "Sporty Carpenter." (At that time, Carpenter had just come off that phenomenal record of 56–10–1 that he racked up from 1973 to 1978.)

"Great! I'd like to speak with him about the possibility of having him motivate these managers into coalescing as a team," Smith replied.

"Sporty is a football coach, not a manager," said Smith's astonished colleague.

Smith, understanding that the fundamentals of teamwork are the same in all activities, pursued the project of bringing Sporty to Little Rock for the project.

On a wet spring day in 1980, the managers were assembled in a retreat on Lake Conway where Sporty held them in rapture with his discussion about how to set goals, put together strategies and tactics, how to exploit the skills of colleagues toward the common goal, and how to communicate and adapt during the action of the day.

Smith reported that Sporty's schedule would not allow him to remain with the group as long as they all wanted, but his effect on the managers was inspirational and enduring. According to Smith, the walls between departments began to fall almost immediately. Managers, who previously were reluctant to share information, communicated effectively and even began to give their peers a heads-up about potential problems during the daily news cycle.

"While Sporty was a spectacular football coach, he could have just as easily become a spectacular business executive because the process of building teams that worked smoothly and effectively was definitely burned into his DNA. Moreover, the results he helped me create made me look far better than I was," said Smith, who now works as a news media consultant in the Washington, D.C., area.

Paul "Sweet Meat" Dixon

Teammate

Sporty came to HSU when I was a junior, maybe sophomore, I played with him two years. I was at Henderson from 1952 till 1955.

When Sporty was coaching at Wynne he taught a special education type class. He had an old boy that wasn't too sharp so he gave him a one-question oral test. He asked him, "Who assassinated JFK?" The boy thought a long time and answered, "Lance Allworth." Sporty grinned and said, "That's close enough, Hoss, you passed."

Dwight Adams

Teammate

An emotional Adams recounted the day Coach Carpenter died. "Sporty called me the day he died and said, 'looks like I'm going to make it boy, just called to say I love you.'" Dwight goes on to say Ronnie Kerr was in the room and got on the phone to tell Dwight that Sporty was fading in and out. He died later that day.

Randy Hornbeck

Football player

Oh gosh, Coach Carpenter, I was never sure he knew my name, he always called me Hallbrook! The offensive coordinator always called me Randy Bradley from Hornbeck but I knew that he and the other coaches cared about me.

Coach Carpenter was one of those types of guys who always had an open door, you always knew that you could go in and talk to him. I never took the opportunity to do that very often. I would go in with some other guys and visit but seldom went in alone. I was not a very good player; I never touched the field until my junior year when I got to punt some. Still, in practice when I might kick the ball well during a drill Coach Carpenter would sidle up next to me and make a positive comment like, you got that one down to about the twenty, that legs getting strong! When you are not a starter or one of the main players you never really think the coaches know you that well, but he did.

I'll never forget the year I was a student assistant after I had played out my eligibility and we had the first pep rally in Day Armory and Coach Carpenter introduced all the coaches but he did not mention my name and it kind of hurt my feelings but after naming all the coaches he started telling this story about this guy and I'm listening but I have not a clue as to who he is talking about. The guy he is describing lost his job on the team his senior year but continued to keep his head up and practice hard and never complain. At the end of the year he won his job back and contributed and he said, "That's what I remember about Coach Hornbeck." I was completely stunned when he said that. I had no idea he would ever use me to inspire or motivate others. It was an honor.

Once I asked him to make a phone call for me in reference to a job down in Austin, Texas, for which I had applied. I just happened to be near his office one day when he actually made the call on my behalf and I still don't know who that guy was he was describing! He made me sound like I was the greatest coach ever. I was overwhelmed that he would go to bat for me so strongly when I never really contributed to the team on the field. It shows to me the depth and breadth of his character. After twenty-eight years of coaching and coaching guys like me you really realize the impact one's coaches had on your life.

Raymond "Rayho" Etheridge
Teammate and friend

I went to school in Hamburg with Sporty up until the ninth grade, and then I moved to Crossett. When we came to Henderson I was his roommate. We go back a long ways. Sporty got the nickname Sporty while attending a Boy Scout camp; I think it was near Magnolia. They had a skit during the camp and Sporty had a part in which he had a rope around his neck and was crying, "Water, master, water!"

We grew up in Hamburg; I knew his mom and dad and his sister and brother. They lived near Hamburg and we just had fun, riding horses and skinny dipping and eating watermelons and so forth. He always had a smile on his face and he always had something humorous to say.

Sporty loved Coach Wells, of course, and Coach Wells noticed that Sporty only weighed 165 pounds, but he was tougher than a pine knot! Sporty called Coach Wells the Duke of Paducah, although, not to his face.

When he and Sabra first married, we kept up with each other, visiting and such; he was a gracious guy who gave of himself freely.

Craig Fant
Football player

I have a couple of things about Coach Carpenter that are pretty funny.

The first time me and a couple of guys came up to HSU on a "recruiting" trip from Linden, we were ushered into Coach Carpenter's little corner office and he was sitting there behind his small desk looking at us like we were crazy. Someone introduced us to him and he told us to sit down. After staring at us for what seemed like five minutes in silence, he looked at Andy Smith and said, "Hmmm ... Smith ... that sure is a common name." We all nervously laughed and said yes sir. Well we went on and visited for a few minutes and he told me I was "the man" after I had told him my ACT score and he gave me some paperwork to fill out and dismissed us to Jeff Atkinson, who showed us around campus, telling us to come back in about a month for a spring ball game. A month or so later, I called and told Coach Carpenter my name and asked if he remembered who I was and could I come watch that Saturday's scrimmage. He quickly replied, "Yeah, you are that big square-headed boy from Linden; we go to war at 10 A.M. Saturday. Be here at 9:30!" I knew at that point HSU was the place for me!

A couple of years later we made a big overnight road trip to Panhandle State in far-western Oklahoma. We spent that Friday night at a hotel somewhere about halfway across the state. Feeling good about being on a big road trip and getting to play a little, I thought I had hit the big time. We had a buffet dinner that night that had chicken fried steak and all the trimmings, so I loaded my plate down with two of them. I sat down not far from where the coaches were and was about to dig in, big-time college football player that I was. All of a sudden Coach Carpenter very loudly starts reprimanding me about having so much food on my plate! The whole team is giggling as he is smoking me about eating so much. He looked over to someone and said, "Be dang sure this one never makes another road trip!" I was devastated and felt about two inches tall. I had ruined my chance at the big time and was upset all night. The next morning I came out my room and was heading to breakfast and I happened to bump in to Coach Carpenter. He smiled, giggled, and said, "Fant, let's be sensible about our eating this morning!" I felt a whole lot better and made a couple of tackles, and much to my relief was lucky enough to be on my travel squad the rest of my career.

Those kinds of things are what made it fun to play for Coach Carpenter and the Reddies!

Reggie Spieghts
Football player, 1967–1970, and friend

When I came to Henderson Sporty was the offensive line coach and Coach Clyde Berry was the head coach. Coach Carpenter was always kidding people but he was serious on the field. He got angry with me several times when we were doing board drills with his offensive line. My strategy on the board drill was to avoid contact if I could and make the tackle. Sporty wanted me to be a target for his dogs and he would yell for me to "stay on the boards!" Sporty loved his offensive linemen, he loved his dogs and took extremely good care of them, seeing to it that they got good equipment and always were prepared to do their best.

There are all kinds of stories about Sporty and the football dorm, he was the dorm daddy and he knew what was going on all the time. He would catch someone violating a rule and at the proper time, he would come in and make sure the perpetrator was properly oriented.

The one thing about Coach Sporty Carpenter that stands out in my mind is the fact that he would help you in any way he could if you needed help. I graduated from Henderson in 1970 and at that time I wasn't sure if wanted to coach so I went back to Smackover and went back to working on that oil rig I had worked on all the time I was in college. During that time that I was working on that oil rig that summer, Sporty called me one night and said, "Reginall, what are you doing?" I said that I was working on an oil rig, making pretty good money. He said, "Well, I got you a coaching job and all you got to do is show up, you won't even have to interview for the job." The job was at Rockwall, Texas. It was with a coach that Coach Carpenter had coached with at Wynne. I think his name was Roy

Hall. Sporty told me he had coached with Roy and all you have to do is show up and you have a coaching job, pack your bags and you can start coaching. I told him then that I just didn't want to get into the coaching game and I turned down the offer. As I have said before, Sporty loved to help people. When I started with South West we weren't doing any business with Henderson and Coach Carpenter immediately started buying a few things from us and in a couple of years I started calling on Sporty and he bought more and more, not all, but he threw us a bone so to speak and it really helped us at the time.

Rex Nelson
OBU sports information director and friend

I was a bit worried when I became the sports editor of Arkadelphia's *Daily Siftings Herald* as a college freshman. Anyone connected with the rivalry between Henderson and Ouachita knows how heated it is. As sports editor, I would cover both schools. And I was determined to do it well. But in a small town where everyone knows each other, everyone indeed knew I bled purple and gold. I had grown up one block from Ouachita's football field, running the sidelines at Tiger games since I was old enough to walk.

I was a freshman at Ouachita. I was part of the Ouachita broadcasting team. But I was also to cover the Reddies.

How was Coach Carpenter going to treat me? He was, of course, going to treat me like a professional, but not without a lot of good-natured ribbing in the process.

I had written a profile of Ouachita's head coach, Buddy Benson, in which I pointed out that Benson had played at the University of Arkansas for Bowden Wyatt and that Wyatt had played at the University of Tennessee for the legendary General Bob Neyland. That, I contended, made Benson a direct football descendant of

General Neyland. Coach Carpenter had a nickname for everyone. I was always Rexall. In my presence, Coach Carpenter began referring to Coach Benson as the General.

Each time I would show up at a Henderson practice, Coach Carpenter would say something along the lines of: "What is the General up to today?" Or "Did the General send you over here to spy on us?"

The best moments, though, would come when gathering quotes after a game.

Once after a Reddie tailback had fumbled late in a crucial game at home, Coach Carpenter described him to me as a "triple threat— a threat to the opposition, a threat to us and a threat to himself."

I wasn't there for the famous game in Monticello when Coach Carpenter stated that "lightning struck the outhouse and we were in it."

But I was there two years later when the Boll Weevils again upset the Reddies.

This time, he told me: "Rexall, it was a total waste of time. We would have been better off to stay home, parch peanuts, and watch the Mandrel sisters on TV."

Robert Hester
Football player

Coach Baker, I'm sorry for the delay on responding back to you. I have been unable to find the picture you asked about and these are the only two I have found so far. I will send others later if I find them. The picture of the kicking team from left to right is Richard Pryor, Greg Magee, Billy Meeks, Joe Smith, Robert Hester, and Wilber Hunter or Jasper Benton sometime in 1974. The other one is me and Coach Bock in 1975 or 1976.

I know there are so many stories we all have to share about

Coach Carpenter and I really appreciate what you are doing and know it will be great.

First and foremost I believe Coach Carpenter was a wonderful person who sincerely cared about all his players and coaches. As successful as his teams were during my five years at Henderson I believe he was as proud of the number of his players that received their degrees as he was of the AIC championships. We all remember having to check in for breakfast every day of the year and wondered why. I know in my heart it was his way of seeing that we were up and would make it to class. You did not want him pointing you out for skipping class in front of the group or having to run the fifty bleachers for missing breakfast or class.

I do not believe I would have been at Henderson if not for him much less have completed my degree there. As a recruit he was the one that talked J. B. Grimes and me into coming. I was at fullback my first year and during spring training. I was depressed and really confused about what I wanted to do. I decided I would quit the team and went to Coach Carpenter with my decision. He did not try and talk me out of it, just wished me the best in his caring way. After one night in Newberry I knew I had made a terrible mistake and wondered if he would let me back on the team. We met that morning and I asked him to let me back on the team and please move me to linebacker where I knew in my heart I could play. He was unbelievably nice and supportive about the whole situation, never making me feel like a quitter or loser, which I would have been that day and from then on. Thirty-five years later looking back over that one day, I honestly believe it was the turning point in my life and wonder where I would be today if not for Sporty Carpenter.

We all to this day wonder how and where he got all his info on everything that was going on around the dorm, campus, off campus, and anywhere else his players might be. He knew things about each of us that there was no way you thought he would have any idea about, much less know, but he would. I remember receiving several calls from him and he would only say you better straighten out this or that. He then would hang the phone up and never say another word about it.

It seemed he had a nickname for everyone or just called you by your last name. I remember reading articles in the paper and he would tell the sportswriter my nickname was Thumper, Tombstone, etc. Whatever he made up at that time and all I remember him calling me in person was either Hess or Hester and, of course, Hoss Fly.

I believe many will remember the day in spring practice when we were having our usual goal-line scrimmage and the offense was having a tough time of it. Coach Mills came into the huddle and told us to let them score or we may be here all day. We did, and after the play, Coach Carpenter looked around and stated, "Coach, I smell a rat," and we had no idea he could kick a ball so far up the hill with those bird legs of his. Of course, we were there for a while that day.

Coach Baker, you told me you did not remember his speech in Vienna, Austria, that night. My mother was there and she sure remembers. It was after our first night there and we had the twenty-four-hour bus ride from West Berlin. There was no curfew but we were to all be on the bus the next morning at a specific time and you know how he was about being on time. We came in at all hours during the night and many of us were not in our assigned rooms the next morning and after rousing everyone out we were at least thirty minutes late leaving for the scheduled practice. We all thought we were back in two-a-days with all the running we did that morning and he did not say anything at the time. That night after supper we had a team meeting with the whole HSU delegation including the girls that were cheerleaders. Sporty got up and stated how disappointed he was in us and he was not naive enough not to think we would not go out and drink a few beers, but to try and drink a whole city dry in one night, no way. Then he told the girls if they were going to hustle any (blink and blank) it better be one in this room. You could have heard a pin drop and we were wondering who might get a ticket back to the States and of course the rest of the trip there was a curfew and room checks. Over all, it was a great three weeks and a wonderful experience for all of us.

I could go on and on about Sporty as each of us could. What I now appreciate about Coach Carpenter is my knowledge of how many lives he touched and how much better off many of us are because of him. He took a many a chance on a bunch of us. Helped many and made sure they got a degree and then helped find jobs which have led to many careers. I never remember him or any of his staff cursing a player even when tempers were at a peak and talking with players from other schools this is very unusual and I think this is a tribute to the man. He always made time to talk and listen to you about personal matters while you were playing for him and even after you were gone.

The past twenty years since his death have flown by very fast but it only seems like yesterday when we were on the field and he was blowing his whistle on the practice field or on the side line in his gray pants, white shirt, and red sweater or vest. I know he is look-ing down with that chew in his mouth and smiling about the day we will see each other again.

Once again, thanks, Coach Baker.

Ron Brazell
Football player

This story starts in the spring semester of my Jr year. I had enrolled in ROTC to get my grade point up with no intentions of ever join-ing the army. Let alone as an officer. Part of the curriculum for ROTC during your junior year is a course to teach the cadets how to conduct Army Physical Training. The course start time was 0600

(6:00 A.M.) three days a week. This was a mandatory course if you were a junior in the program. I figured since I played football I would have no problem with something as easy as Army Physical Training. I showed up for about 50 percent of the classes prior to spring football starting up. The class consisted of a two- to five-mile run coupled with a lot of push-ups, sit-ups, pull-ups, and a variety of other like type exercises. No problem for a football player, right? Well, once spring football kicked off I decided on my own that I was no longer going to show up for the ROTC Physical Training Course and explained to the instructor that I didn't have to attend his course, I was a football player in spring training. Everything went along real well for about two weeks. One day I got a message from one of the managers that Coach Carpenter wanted to see me before the next practice. I was thinking no big deal he probably wants to talk about how much I had improved over the spring training. As you can guess that was not the discussion we were going to have. I showed up in his office and there sat my ROTC instructor and Coach Carpenter. Coach started with "Boy, I understand you can't make it to PT with the ROTC class because you are a football player." The conversation went south from there. I ended up not only doing the Physical Training Course with ROTC, I got the opportunity to run hills before each practice and run bleachers after each practice for the remainder of the spring semester, all the time with Coach Carpenter right there explaining the lessons in life as I did my time on the hill. His biggest lesson was that football is not an excuse, it was attitude and feeling that you had inside that one should carry for the rest of his life. Relying on it when times got hard . . . kind of like running those bleachers after every practice . . .

Story two starts in the second semester of my junior year. We'll call this one the "accidental commissioning." It's fall and with fall football comes two-a-days and the start of the new season. Once again I was enrolled in ROTC to get my grade point up with no intentions of ever going into the army. This semester I was going to take only twelve hours so I could focus on the fall football season. Again, two-a-days went as well as two-a-days have ever went, running the "Gassers" until every freshman on the squad was on their knees puking and wondering what they had gotten themselves into. The season started off great and everything was clicking, getting more game time and enjoying the season. About the middle of the semester I was sitting in English class and there was a knock on the door. It was the ROTC instructor and he wanted to talk to me. I was asked to come out in the hall and talk. The ROTC instructor explained that it was time for me to contract and join the army or I would have to drop the course. I explained in no uncertain terms that I was not interested in joining the army and that I would not enroll in next semester classes. Keep in mind I was only taking twelve hours so if I were to drop the course I was not eligible to play football. I refused to sign the contract and thought I had pulled a good one over on the ROTC instructor. Within two hours I had a message that Coach Carpenter wanted to see me before practice. This was a Thursday before a game on Saturday. I thought that Coach was going to discuss with me more game time for the upcoming game. Well, that wasn't the conversation. Again, I walked into his office and there sat the ROTC instructor with all of his paperwork. Coach Carpenter started the conversation with a discussion that went something like this: "Boy, it ain't going to hurt you one damn bit to go in the army, in fact it might just do you some good . . ." He gave me a few stories of his time in the service and some lessons that he had learned. The ROTC instructor laid all his paperwork on the desk and Coach ended the conversation with "besides if you don't sign the contract you can't play the remainder of the season." Well, I signed the contract with much hesitation and was not happy with the way this all transpired. I had no intentions of ever actually joining the army. The time was 1989.

Here we are over twenty years later and I am still an officer in the army. A career that has carried me all over the world to include a rotation in Tikrit, Iraq, during the surge in support of Operation Iraqi Freedom. It has always amazed me how many times the lessons that I learned from each and every coach during my time at Henderson State was applicable in the "real world." I used many of Coach Carpenter's sayings during the deployment and could always find that Reddie spirit inside when things got really hard. When I thought I couldn't take another step or move another inch, I would reach down deep inside and hear those words that I remember hearing as a freshman at the end of my first day of practice, right after Gasser number 12 . . . it was Coach Carpenter yelling, "Get up, boy, you haven't even started playing college football, you've got to want it more than you ever wanted anything. You aren't going to get anything handed to you out here, you are going to have to work for it." And you know again . . . he was right; that lesson applied to life not just that practice field. I would like to thank all of the coaches that were such a big part of my life. I was too young to realize it wasn't just football they were coaching. I would like to give a special thanks to Coach George Baker, Coach Charles Thomas, and Coach Ronnie Efird for your patience and not giving up on me in spite of my attempts to better myself in my own mind.

Well, Coach, that pretty much sums it up from this end. Let me know if you need more info or detail. That is pretty much how I remembered it taking place. Thanks again for the opportunity to contribute to your book.

Ron Freer

IP supervisor

I first had contact with Sporty Carpenter when he contacted me about some of his players working in the IP plant that I had the responsibility of running. I was impressed with the personal interest he took with all of his players trying to get those who needed it employment through the summer months.

We were just starting up the plant and, typically, you get some union activity. Our intent was to manage the plant in such a way that our employees would feel that they didn't need such a union. I talked to Sporty and told him that I didn't know if we could hire many guys because we were in this campaign to defeat the union move. Sporty said, "Don't worry about that, and just let me know how you want these guys to vote." Of course, we didn't use that hole card and defeated the union fair and square, by a three-to-one margin, but I was impressed by his feeling and care for those young men, and with their love for him.

I thought it over and we hired about twenty of Sporty's boys. We continued to hire Reddie football players for the remainder of Sporty's tenure there. His interest, not just in the players but also the university's well-being resulted in our plant donating landscaping bark to go on the campus flowerbeds and all. This was very impressive to me that he saw to interests of the university other than his own area. His involvement with International Paper Company led to the formulation of a scholarship fund for children of our employees that eventually, before we sold the plant to Georgia Pacific, had over $100,000 in it.

Ron Paxton

I came to Henderson from Callahan, Florida, in 1979 and was there for four years. I only played football my freshman and sophomore years. I got hurt my freshman year.

When I think of Coach Carpenter I always remember the meetings in the spring of the year when he had a one-on-one set-to with each player. He would spend forty-five minutes to an hour talking to you and he never mentioned football. He would ask me what are you doing with your life, what do you want to do, etc. That impressed in me that he cared about you more than just football; he cared about you as a student and human being. He was crusty on the outside but soft on the inside like a toasted marshmallow, rough on the exterior but warm and soft on the inside.

When I sustained my injury I continued to practice but when we got to the rough stuff Coach Carpenter would pull me out and sit me down to protect me from further injury. I went into his office, all hang dog mad and depressed because I wasn't getting what I thought was my fair shake. When I walked into his office he looked up and asked, "What's wrong with you, boy?" I said, "Coach, I don't know, it's all in my head." He said, "There ain't anything wrong with your head, it's your leg that is messed up!" He said, "It's going to be two years before you can walk like a regular human being." I said, "I don't know about all that." He leaned back in his chair and smiled and said, "I'm not going to cut you. You can stay on the team as long as you want but I'm not going to let you hit because your knee can't stand another injury." I said, "I understand but if I'm not going to get to play it's too hard and I'm going to go ahead and get started with my life." He said, "I understand and since you will not have a scholarship any more I will help you in any way I can." He said, "I have a job here and you can start tomorrow as a manager." I thanked him but declined because I just didn't think I could hand out jocks to the guys I had been playing with. But that is not the story I wanted to tell, this is: I started out majoring in math and found out that was not what I wanted to do. In one of those face-to-face meetings after I hurt my leg Coach Carpenter asked me what I wanted to do when I grew up. I told him that I might be interested in journalism. That subject never came up again until I hurt my knee and could no longer play. One day my sophomore year Coach Carpenter called me in and told me that he had a job for me in the press box for Henderson football games. I had forgotten about mentioning journalism but he had not. He was trying to help me get a job I wanted. I was no longer a potential athlete but he cared about me as a person. I took this job and it helped me continue my education. I am thankful that I encountered this fine man.

Ronnie and Donnie Braddock
Football players

Ronnie and Donnie Braddock arrived at Henderson State much as I arrived at Ouachita. They were coached in high school down in Callahan, Florida, by a Henderson graduate from Arkadelphia named Jim Stern. Coach Stern was and is a loyal Reddie. He, as mentioned earlier, is probably directly and indirectly responsible for more football prospects attending his alma mater than anyone else I know. His first two players to show up in Arkadelphia were Troy Tison and George Baker, both of whom walked on and made the team, graduated and moved on to good, productive lives, and all the better from having met this good man. Troy and I played on Coach Stern's first football teams beginning in 1958 and graduating in 1961, his last year at Clinch County High School. Coach Stern moved that year to Green Cove Springs High School, right outside of Jacksonville, Florida. He was there for two years before he moved to Callahan and met the Braddock brothers.

The Braddock brothers almost defy description! They are rough and tumble in personality and are possessed of a passion for life and football that has endured for almost forty years. In discussing them

Sporty would always use the term "they refuse to turn down a phys-ical challenge." They grew up in the gut-wrenching labor of the southern log woods, an occupation that is an icon for hard labor. Anything one attempts after working in this environment is consid-ered easier. You may name army boot camp, easier, marine training, easier, Ranger school, easier. It is dangerous and unforgiving; one slip of the foot and disaster can strike one down. A moment of inat-tention can be fatal. Ronnie and Donnie escaped the log woods the exact way as did I—football.

Clyde Berry was the head football coach when the Braddock twins arrived on campus. They first met R. L. Sporty Carpenter when they checked into the football dorm. He and Sabra were new to the staff and were the dorm daddy and mom. David was a kid and fell in with this rowdy bunch and was overeducated immediately.

Time and space will not allow me to cover all the Braddock antics so I will just relate a few of my favorites.

As luck would have it, the Braddocks' freshman year was a year of unusual difficulty. Coach Berry, another coach who refused to allow an opponent to out work him, decided to have four-a-day practices. I refer to this type of planning as an adaption of the four-aspirin theory. If two aspirins every four hours are good, then why not take four aspirins ever two hours? Besides being a staff killer there is just not enough hours in a day to have four practices. Coach Berry's method was in part an attempt to deal with way too many show ups. At any rate the plan called for splitting the squad into two teams and working each team twice. Ronnie got hurt; he and Donnie had been split and were on a different schedule. They were both trying out for scholarships and both would prove later that they could play. Donnie, an identical twin, took Ronnie's place and also worked his shifts. An incredible sacrifice as anyone who has been through two-a-day football practice will attest. They are tough, brash, physically in your face with no regard for their body, and that just partially paints a picture of this pair of warriors. They soon caught the attention of their position coach, the great Charlie Donaldson. Charlie was one of Henderson's first All-Americans and a legend in his own right. To this day, forty-odd years later, the Braddocks speak with reverence when they speak of Charlie. They call him Coach, never by his given name. Coach Carpenter held Charley in much the same regard. He called him, Chally, but to his dying day Coach Carpenter thought Chally was the best defensive coach in America.

Ronnie recently told me this short story to illustrate their relationship with Coach Carpenter.

This incident occurred after the twins had established themselves as starters and it happened during a hot early fall practice. Coach Carpenter asked Chally to send him two linebackers to fill in a drill he had set up for his dogs. The dogs were inexperienced those years, being mostly freshmen and sophomores. Ronnie chortled that he and Donnie were killing them, knocking them off the boards and savaging the running backs unlucky enough to be in the màlee. He said that Sporty stopped the drill and yelled down to Chally, "Chally, take these two a&*%#@*s back down there and send me two chitlins!" Translated, chitlins are easy picking.

One last story that must be told concerns a request by Coach Carpenter for a parrot. Donnie attended medical school in the Dominican Republic and when Coach Carpenter learned that parrots were plentiful there he asked Donnie to bring him one. Donnie promised he would get the coach a bird and in the fashion of the twin's courage Donnie proceeded to do just that. He obtained a parrot, gave the parrot a large dose of sleeping pills, and concealed the bird underneath his shirt. Unfortunately, he miscalculated the amount of drug needed and the parrot woke up just as Donnie was about to pass through customs. Donnie said, "George, I hated to do it but I had to break the parrot's neck." But he did, losing his investment for that try. On his next trip Donnie allowed for all stops; layovers, delays, etc., and administered the correct dosage and got the bird to Sporty on his next trip to Arkadelphia. The bird was in Sporty's home until his death.

I know of no alumni who are more loyal than the Braddock twins. I don't think they have missed a year since their graduation in which they did not return to Arkadelphia or catch the Reddie football team somewhere nearer to Callahan to add their support. They typically charge into the dressing room unannounced, yelling, "Give 'em hell, Reddies!" They then proceed in giving a pep talk to the team and their speaking skills are considerable. They never fail to emote great passion and verve, at least for the moment. The Braddock twins were solely responsible for recruiting the great Joe Smith to Henderson State, a deed that has had far-reaching impact. They have worked tirelessly over the years, sending many, many athletes to their alma mater.

Ronnie Bailey
Friend and teammate at HSU

I started to Henderson in the fall of 1954. One of the first characters I met was Sporty Carpenter. We were both at the back of the calisthenics formation. This was a matter of survival so we could rest a little under the watchful eyes of Coach Wells and Coach Sawyer. We had both been in the navy and not in the greatest physical condition. They say misery loves company, so we naturally were drawn to share our misery or discomfort.

One summer, Sporty, John Greenwood, and I got a job teaching swimming at Haygood Pool. I'm not sure Sporty could swim. We stayed waterlogged and had turned green from that over chlorinated pool. I think we made $1.25 per hour.

In the fall of 1957, Sporty went to Shawnee High School in Joiner, Arkansas, to coach football. The following year he joined me at Liberty-Eylau High School in Texarkana, Arkansas. In 1959 our team won twelve games in a row and went to the state quarter finals.

Sporty was a great asset to our team. He was the line coach and did a super job. He loved the seven-man sled and nearly wore it out the first year we got it.

Sporty was the head boys' basketball coach. We always went to the Henderson Invitational Tournament, but didn't last past the first game.

Sporty liked to be mobile and so he moved a lot. One day he moved two or three houses down from his house. He had no dolly to move his refrigerator so he dragged it across his neighbor's lawn on a quilt.

Sporty was a big-hearted guy, always willing to help players. If you, as a coach, had a prospect that needed help to go to school and play football, Sporty would give them a chance. Two of my former players went to Henderson and played for the Reddies. Sporty gave them a chance and it paid off.

He was a player's coach and could always get the best out of a player. You might call him a diamond in the rough. What you saw was what you got. He was unique and I am proud to have had him as a friend. They threw away the mold when they made him. I'll always miss him and Sabra. I'm glad to know his son David is carrying on his winning tradition.

Author's note: Coach Carpenter held Ronnie Bailey in highest regard. He would proudly say, "Ronnie Bailey was the first real hippie I ever saw!"

Spriggs Nutt
Friend, fellow coach

Spriggs Nutt goes way back with Coach Carpenter. He and Sporty coached at Wynne, Arkansas, and even before that when Sporty was the manager for the basketball program at Henderson when Spriggs played for the team. Spriggs remembers the aplomb with which Sporty handled the difficulty of that first losing season at Wynne. He used humor with each situation. Sporty was always the life of the party and would say or do something to get you motivated. Cliff Garrison and I lived together in an apartment in Wynne, and Sporty would come and get us every Saturday morning to go to the coffee shop to drink coffee with the local boosters, or "wolves," as he called them. If we lost, which we did eight times that year, Sporty would claim, bad breaks and crooked referees will get you every time!

I remember one year in Wynne he got me to go to the Dan Devine coaching clinic at the University of Missouri. I said, "Sporty, I can only help you early in the season before basketball starts and I don't know anything about football. You don't need to take me up there." Sporty said, "Don't worry, we are going to party." That was in the early sixties and we ended up going to some beatnik place where we had to sit on the floor and listen to hippies recite poetry and burn candles and smoke dope. Oh Lord, I thought we would never get out of there. We were out of our medium to say the least. We were so happy to get away from the hippies that we got on the wrong road. He made me drive and we got lost on some gravel road somewhere up there on the Missouri line and ran out of gas. We were having such a great time talking about things that we had forgot to buy gas for the car. I got out and hailed a couple down and they brought us a can of gas and saved us from having to walk a long way.

People in Wynne loved him, even though we had a tough year that first year. He kept everything going. Later, after I left Wynne to coach basketball at Sparkman, he called me up and told me he was interviewing for a job at Bearden and if he got the job he wanted me to be the basketball coach there. At that time he was the assistant coach at Magnolia or somewhere. He wanted me to go interview with him, he said, "Get one of your ties and pack your pasteboard box, we are gonna go to Bearden for an interview." I said, "Sporty, they don't care anything about basketball at Bearden, that's a football school! You would be in good, but I wouldn't." Sporty said, "It's the sleeping giant of the South. You will win in basketball, I know it!" I said, "No, I am not going."

There are lots of stories I could tell you about Sporty. He was a great motivational type guy as you well know. He kept me in stitches all the time. You never had a dull moment when he was around!

His influence was not just in football; all the kids in school loved him. He would get kids out of study hall where they were flunking classes and just vegetating as he called it, and get them to work for us in athletics. The effect of that interest motivated many a failing student to go on and graduate, and many of them went to college. Alvin Futtrell is one who benefited from Sporty's interest. Alvin was smart and a good student, but didn't realize his potential until Sporty motivated him and helped him.

Those were great years and we later were on the staff at Henderson for a while. Sporty continued to support me and kept me in his circle long after I left Henderson.

Steve "Pup" Eddington
Sports information director and friend

Steve Eddington worked closely with Coach Carpenter and was dubbed "Pup" for the boundless energy he displayed as the sports information director for the Reddie sports programs. Recently, Steve took time from his busy day as director of public relations for Arkansas Farm Bureau to relate the following account of one of his memories of Coach Sporty Carpenter.

Steve: I happened into Sporty's office one afternoon in the middle of a counseling session Coach was having with a young man, who will remain anonymous for obvious reasons. The atmosphere was scorching, to say the least. Sporty was putting the heat on the young man who had a severe speech impediment. The session lasted for several uncomfortable minutes and eventually the young man was released with an admonition to "do better!"

After the fellow was out of ear shot I asked Sporty if the guy was a prospect to help the team. Sporty leaned back and spat a large stream of tobacco into the trash can between his legs and replied, "No, but I just want to help him to be the best he can be."

That account epitomizes the feelings R. L. Carpenter had for the student athletes in his charge. The young man did not remain on the team for very long but left the program all the better for his experience. Steve and I witnessed that scenario in various hues many times during our ride with R. L. Carpenter.

Terrance Anthony "TAB" Brown
Football player

I thought Coach Carpenter was a fair man, to me he was much like an uncle, daddy, or old man as anything. I want to talk about him in a couple of ways, one, the last time I saw him and, two, the first time I met him.

The last time I saw him he was in the hospital in Memphis waiting on a transplant. The day he passed, Wayne Davenport, my brother Scotty, Tyrone Forte, and I were all coming to the hospital to see him. I had seen him two or three days the week before he passed, down in the transplant center. He called me early that week and told me he couldn't find a *Democrat-Gazette* so I would pick up one and take it to his room and then go on to work. I didn't see him the day of his operation, and when I arrived home that day Scotty and the guys were at my home and told me he had died.

In the hospital he was Coach, calling you boy and telling you to come here and do this or hurry up and do this, etc. "Go over there and get me a *Gazette,*" "these people don't have the *Gazette* here," you know, just like he was still coaching me. That was Coach. I felt as much compelled to do his bidding as I felt honored that he would ask me.

I spent four and a half years with Coach, from the time I was seventeen until I was twenty-two, a significant portion of my life and a very important segment of my life. When I saw him in the hospital he was very happy that I had a job and I was happy that he was happy! He felt that way about all his boys. I miss him.

The first time I saw Coach I had met Coach Massey when he visited my high school but I had no idea if Henderson really wanted me or was just including me in the mix to get some other player from my school. When I came down to Henderson for a visit I met Coach Carpenter in his office. He told me to get with the guys he had assigned to show me around and get out on the campus and find a reason to want to come to school at HSU! Go find something you like and come on over here. I thought that was a profound way to put it, go find something you like!

We went up to the dorm and Fred Williams and Terrance White cooked for us and it just felt like home. I liked and loved it so much at Henderson that I did not go home after my freshman year until I had no more classes left, just my practice teaching. Henderson had become my home and Coach Carpenter had become as much family to me as anyone.

I don't quite know how to describe Coach Carpenter, my mom liked Coach, and he just had a down-home type of personality. He would come into my home and sit down with my parents and just talk, not about football but about my future and the future of my brother, Scotty. Scotty also attended Henderson State and he also graduated. My mother always felt as if she gave Henderson two fine boys and Henderson returned two fine men. Coach Carpenter became my surrogate parent and he saw to our needs while we studied and played football and Scotty became a manager for the team. We were happy and we gained good educations that will benefit us all of our lives. Much of the credit for this profound thing goes to Coach Carpenter.

Author's note: TAB's dad was the great Bob Brown, who played for Vince Lombardi in the first Super Bowl.

Terry Blaylock
Football player

In 1974, we played UAM in Monticello! We were in the film room on Sunday watching film with the offense. The play is a fake blast off tackle, tight end drag route across the field in the opposite direction. I make my fake, Joe Yancy is our tight end, he runs the drag, I throw the ball and it hits Joe in the face mask and of course he does not catch it. Coach Cerato keeps running the play back and forth pointing out mistakes, etc., you know how long we used to have to stay in film versus the defense. Coach Carpenter finally asks Joe what the hell was wrong with that pass. Joe wore glasses back then under the helmet and he had forgotten to bring them so he was blind as a bat. He tells Coach he had forgotten his glasses and that all he could see was a blur! Coach Carpenter says, "Hell, Josephus, next time catch the damn blur!!!"

Tommy Wilson
Baseball player, graduate assistant

Stories about Sporty
Football: Pryor and Green in dorm hall. When I was a senior, I was the athletic dorm counselor. One night we had beaten cross-town rival

Ouachita in a "B" game. After the game Lewis Pryor was in the dorm hall and about thirty yards down the hall was a guy named Green who had caught the game-winning pass from Pryor. Everyone was excited. Pryor yelled at Green and dropped back down the hall. Green was demonstrating how he caught the winning touchdown pass. Pryor let loose a make-believe pass and Green jumped toward an open doorway. As he was going to make the make-believe catch he hit his head against the top of the door frame. Blood went everywhere. We rushed him to the hospital emergency room. He had to have ten stitches to close the cut. I called Sporty and he got to the hospital and just stood there shaking his head when he heard how it happened. He said, "Hoss, we got too many injuries in games and practice to be getting hurt in the dang dorm hallway."

Baseball: Southern Arkansas trip concerning bus breaking down. We were on the way home from playing at Southern Arkansas in the fairly new college transit bus. About ten miles from Gurdon the engine in the rear started smoking up the inside of the bus and finally made a last pop and the engine stopped. We coasted to a safe area to pull over. Coach Carpenter asked the driver if he had changed the oil and he said yeah. I walked with coach to a house on a hill. He asked the lady if he could use her phone. He called the college and told them to send some vans to pick us up in Gurdon. He then called a wrecker to come and tow us. We waited for an hour and finally the wrecker showed up. The guy hooked the bus up and towed us all in to the service station. As the guy was turning sharp to the right to go beside the service station, the right part of the a-frame of the wrecker busted out the right windshield of the bus. Coach Carpenter got off the bus and said, "Good God, fellow, what are you doing?" The guy told coach that he was sorry, it was an accident. Coach just shook his head and climbed back on the bus. The guy then pulled the bus and turned back to the left to go behind the service station and the left part of the a-frame smashed out the left windshield of the bus. Sporty jumped off the bus, slammed his hat on the concrete, and said, "Good golly, boy, what is going on?" He shook his head and just sat on the curb mumbling to himself. I told him, "Coach, it will be all right." He said, "Willie, I just don't know how I am going to explain this to the President!!! It looks like we had a head-on!!!" Finally the vans came and we got back home.

Baseball: Sporty meeting with me on the mound against Mankato State. Mankato State had a big-time program. They were on a spring tour playing teams during their break due to the bad weather in Minn. I was pitching that day and was keeping the ball down and throwing a lot of breaking pitches at the knees because they had some great hitters. I threw a couple of curve balls in the dirt and Coach Carpenter called timeout! He called for my catcher, Phillip Allen, to come to the mound with him. Phillip and I looked at each other because the game was going pretty well and I had only given up a few hits. Sporty looked at me and said, "Willie, don't be throwing that fool 'em pitch, just throw that high hard one." He turned around and walked off to the dugout and Phillip and I just laughed and winked at each other. I think I gave up a couple of home runs after that from throwing that high hard one!

Baseball: Sporty's bunt-and-steal signals. In one of our first ball games, we had a bunt situation come up. Sporty was coaching third base and yelled at our batter and motioned bunting the ball on the ground for him to bunt and said, "Put it on the ground, Hoss." Then one time we had our fastest player on first. Sporty yelled from the third base coaching box as he pointed to second, "Get on down there, Hoss." Believe me, I cannot tell you how many times it worked.

Baseball: Sporty dismissing a player from team for team violation. One night in the dorm, Sporty made a surprise visit at about midnight. One of our players who had just hit a couple of home runs came in the dorm with a half-full whiskey bottle on his shoulder. He saw

Sporty and just said, Hey, Sportman." The next morning coach Carpenter called for me and Randy Hughes to meet with him because we were the team captains. He told us in the meeting, "Men I will not tolerate that kind of conduct. I want y'all to meet with him and tell him to clean out his locker because he has DEVORCED HISSELF FROM THE BASEBALL PROGRAM." We went and delivered the message just as it was given to us.

Baseball: Sporty and another coach grabbing each other. Ronnie Kerr, or Kerr-Dog as Coach Carpenter called him, was a graduate assistant when this happened. It was so funny! You may want to talk to Ronnie Kerr about that one.

Sporty helping me get back in school. I attended Henderson in the fall of 1967. I was playing football and baseball. I got my draft notice in January of 1969, my lottery number was fifty. So I knew I was going to Vietnam. I was in great shape and just knew that I would pass the physical. I dropped out of school about three weeks before my physical because I was young and wanted to have some fun before I left. Well, I went on a bus with fifty-six other guys to Little Rock to take the physical. After an all-day deal, the doctors decided that I could not hear a high-pitch sound and my blood pressure was high so they gave me a 1-Y, which meant I failed it. Only three guys out of fifty-six failed the physical. About two days later I got a phone call from Coach Carpenter. He asked, "Willie, how did that physical go?" I told him what happened and he said, "Boy, get your butt back up here now!!!" I said, "Coach, I dropped out of school." He said, "Boy, get back down here tomorrow." I went back the next day and Coach Carpenter got me back in school. I owe him for my thirty-six-year career in school business with twenty-nine years being in school administration including nineteen as a superintendent.

Sporty reacting to me throwing my glove over the dugout and the unbelievable pinch hitter. We were playing Harding University; I was a junior. I had pitched fourteen complete innings and started the fifteenth. The first guy up got to first on an error. The next guy got an infield hit. Sporty came out to the mound and said, "Willie, hoss, you done a good job." He took me out. As I was walking to the dugout I threw my glove over the dugout and stormed to the bench. I was sitting there fuming. Sporty came in the dugout and put his hand on my knee and said, "Willie, go get your glove." I said, "Yes, sir." Mike Hickey was the new pitcher for us. They got a run in the top of the eighteenth inning. In the bottom of the inning, our first two batters got out. Then for some unheard of reason, Sporty called for a FRESHMAN to pinch hit. He had only batted a few times all season. It was the most surprising move because we had seniors on the bench that could have pinch hit. The freshman looked pitiful on the first two pitches. Then he swung as hard as he could and hit a game-tying home run over the fence. The pinch hitter's name was David Ball. We won the ball game in the bottom of the twenty-second inning. After the game I asked Coach Carpenter why he decided to put the freshman in and he told me, "Willie, with a name like Ball he had to be a good baseball player."

I played baseball four years from 1969–1971 and received the leading pitcher award each year. My junior year I made ALL-AIC and led the AIC in wins. We won the AIC championship but lost it due to an ineligible player. Coach Carpenter had taken over as head baseball coach my junior year. He did not know a whole bunch about baseball at the time. We started practicing and right before our first baseball game he asked me to come over to his house. I came in and he gave me a glass of tea. He sat down at the table with me. He said, "Now, Willie, if you were going to make out this starting lineup, who would you put down?" I wrote down the starting lineup and explained to Coach why I would have them batting in that order. After a while he said, we kind of thought the same way. The next day he posted the lineup right before the game and it was identical to the one I had given him. Coach Carpenter did not want anyone to think he did not know how to coach baseball. After the season Coach Carpenter was promoted to head football coach. I think he always felt that being successful as a baseball coach had helped him in getting the football job. Later in 1976, he called me and asked me if I would want to be a graduate assistant. I said sure. So I got my master's and helped with football and baseball in 1976–77.

Summer driver's education. I was getting credit and helping Coach Carpenter with driver's education during that summer. There seemed to be a lot of football players in the class. This one player was about 6'2 and 260 pounds. He was doing a driving drill in which we used a speaker in the car to give directions. This was a reaction drill. He was supposed to go straight at a pylon and at the last second we would tell him right or left and he would turn sharply to miss the pylon. Well, he was going straight at the pylon and was given the command to turn right. First, he turned left then jerked the wheel to the right, lost control of the vehicle and skidded into a concrete island located in the parking lot. He damaged the left front and rear tires by bending their rims. Sporty said, "Look out, hoss!" as the car skidded out of control. We looked at the damage and Sporty had me drive the vehicle to the car dealer and he followed me. The car was going up and down on that one side and looked funny as I drove it down the road. We got to the dealership and he told me he would be right back. When he got back he scratched his head and said, "Boy, I hated to tell him that we had some knucklehead driving one of his new vehicles and crashed it on the driver's education driving course."

Coach Carpenter was a great man. He was an inspiration. He cared about everybody and he did not care who you were, or where you came from, or who your family was. He was always so genuine. I spent one of Coach Carpenter's last nights on this earth with him. He was going to have the liver transplant so I went to Memphis to visit him. David and his mother were there. I asked David if I could go back and see Coach. He took me back and told Coach Carpenter I was there. Coach was lying on a bed and looked over at me with that twinkle in his eyes and said, "Hey, Willie." He said he was going to get that new liver. I told him, yeah, Coach, everything is going to be fine. He had that bright orange iodine all over him. He was hurting really bad. And he said, "Willie, would you do me a favor?" I said, yeah, Coach, anything you want. He said, "Would you just rub my back right here," and he pointed to the spot. I started rubbing his back and he went to sleep. I cried for two days after I heard Coach had passed away. He meant so much not just to me but also to Henderson State University and hundreds of young people whose lives he had touched. Sporty Carpenter will live forever in the memories of everyone who knew him.

Vance Strange
Fellow coach, opposing coach, friend

My thoughts and memories of Coach Carpenter relate to a mentor, teacher, and realist. He was an unpretentious down-to-earth person. You don't forget him ever.

He had a way to explain things that you never forgot the point. He loved his players and treated them like men.

Wayne Wattlington
Football player

It is great to hear from you after all these years. As you can see on my Facebook, I coached for twenty-five years and finally hung it all up last year and now I just teach science in Waco ISD. I truly enjoy coaching, but just got tired of some of the parents. You know how it can be in a small town. In my twenty-five years, I coached on three state finalist football teams, all at Mart, but only won it one time. It has been a great experience, and I'd do it all over again. Now I'm only refereeing volleyball and basketball games to keep from getting that middle age spread!! Lol

It's a great thing that you are writing this book about Sporty. He touched many lives at HSU and it's very well deserved. There are so many things I could say about him and his sayings. I rank him right up there with Lou Holtz with his funny sayings that he was always quick to share! He was instrumental in my getting my first job in Bastrop, Louisiana. Bastrop called HSU needing a coach. I happened to be walking by the offices and he called me over and asked, "Son, do you need a job?" I said yes and he sent me and two others down to Bastrop. I was the only one that actually had played football in college, I think that helped me. I was hired by the time I left. Then I called him two years later looking for a job. He asked me where I wanted to go; I said I "didn't care as long as I had a job." His comment . . . "Go west, young man, that is where the money is, go to Texas, some good football down there." He me told of several schools, and I applied at Mart HS and about four others. Mart hired me on the spot, after my interview. Don't know if he knew anyone here or not, but I know he knew LOTS of people. He called me a few times asking if we had anyone that could help you guys out at HSU and I would give him a few names but no one ever went 'cause it was "too far away from home for them." They just thought they were football players, had they really wanted to play, they would have gone.

While coaching here at Mart and in Waco, I met up with Jerry Malone. He was coaching at Marlin HS. He has sent several of his athletes to HSU to play football. They have a good program there at Marlin, too. He left Marlin this past year and I'm not exactly sure where he is now. There have been several others—guys, girls that played at HSU—that are down in this area.

CHAPTER THREE

Europe, the Trip of a Lifetime

We were still licking our wounds in the months after Ouachita beat us 21–20 and knocked us out of an undefeated season. There was little solace in beating East Central Oklahoma in the ill-fated, one-time, Aluminum Bowl in Little Rock in 1976. The Tigers were too local and the happenstance of meeting them daily and seeing the gleam of victory in their eyes was almost unbearable! One has to live the agony of defeat by a nearby rival to know the bitter pill that is forced down your throat at each encounter in the small world of Arkadelphia, Arkansas. The truth is that the whole spectrum of this unique nearness is motivated by love not hate. I am often amused by the opining of the unaware when they use "hated rival" to describe one or the other of these two wonderful institutions. "Heated rival" is nearer to the truth but in reality, our proximity breeds familiarity, which in turn breeds admiration! Athletes tend to group with and identify with other athletes. I have spent a total of almost fifty years on the two campuses, and I have been involved with more OBU/HSU games than almost anyone else alive. In my opinion, there is an almost family-like atmosphere between the athletes of the various teams. Many played either against each other in high school or actually were from the same high school teams. The heat of the rivalry comes from a blood/kin connection. Whatever the chemistry, the bottom line is an all-out effort when the two schools compete.

Having said all that, as we dolefully shuffled around the campus bemoaning what could have been, word came that the NAIA was contemplating sending four football teams on a tour of Europe! Did we dare hope that we would get to go? Early on the plan was rumored to be a four-team junket with a rotating schedule and that sounded good. Texas A & I had won the championship and the final ranking included A & I, Henderson State, Salem West Virginia, and Ouachita, in that order. In Arkadelphia, both Ouachita and Henderson figured in that scenario. Coach Carpenter immediately went into high gear, getting okays from all levels of the Henderson hierarchy and generally going about planning for the trip. Ouachita did the same. The administrators of the NAIA were pretty close to the vest for a while but eventually leaks appeared and the rumors really started flying. The teams were going to be allowed seventy-five slots per party. Only individuals who were eligible to play in the fall of 1976 would be allowed to participate on the trip. That left out the seniors from the team, guys who were most responsible for our being in position to enjoy this great adventure. It just didn't seem right but, as we say, that was the way it was!

At that time spring training for football was confined to the month of February. The reason for this was that most AIC track programs were bolstered by football players. February in Arkansas is probably the worst month weatherwise for any type of outdoor activity, but we had no choice. We went into spring practice with our usual vengeance. We had no official notice that we would actually be a part of the European trip.

Sometime during spring training we got the word. We were, indeed, going to be a part of the plan and to their dismay, Ouachita was not going. The sponsors of the trip had researched travel, food, lodging, etc., for four parties of seventy-five and had not liked the result. They had modulated to two teams of seventy-five plus a few NAIA top dogs.

The important thing to us was that we were in the mix! We were going to Europe! Ouachita was not! Poetic justice, we thought, the better team had prevailed. We fought the urge to goody them but it was difficult.

We soon began to get glimpses of the plan. How many players could we take, who else would be eligible to go, time frames, locations, and a myriad of mind-boggling information that was hard to absorb in so short a time.

Still, even though it appeared to be a solid fact that we were going we could not believe our good fortune! They were going to give each player and coach a stipend to defray costs. A godsend for most of our players who were able to attend college only by the happenstance of a football scholarship. PELL grant recipients were not eligible to participate in scholarship sports at that time. This was an NAIA rule and it was soon to be declared illegal, but that is another story in which R. L. Carpenter's vision stood out.

The stipend turned out to be only fifteen dollars a week, but it was all some of the guys had in the way of spending money.

The day of departure finally came and we were loading the bus that was to carry us to the airport. Hijacking was in its early days but still a threat and Coach Carpenter was careful to warn the players to refrain from making jokes about this unfunny subject. As the guys lumbered on the bus we spotted a defensive back from Florida getting on the bus with a duffle bag with the words "time bomb" written plainly on the side of the bag. His position coach, Bradley Mills, reacted appropriately and yelled at the offending player, "What in the hell do you think you are doing with that written on your bag?" The young man, completely and honestly remorseful, responded that his nickname with his teammates was "Time Bomb." "Not on this trip, boy," Coach Mills bellowed in his best coaching voice. "Take this magic marker and blot that out." We were not out of the parking lot and we already had a faux pas. It was one of the few little slips of decorum that were to happen on the three-week whirl of strange new places and things we were to see.

We boarded a 727 stretch jet in Little Rock, Arkansas, and flew nonstop to Houston, Texas.

The A & I football team boarded there . . . The trip to Houston was quiet; our players knew our travel rules and generally obeyed them to a tee. The nature of the blend changed when A & I came into the picture. They were much larger than were we. They had one tackle that was almost seven feet tall and he wore cowboy boots and a large Stetson hat that made him look ten feet tall. He needed two seats but squeezed into one. The noise level soared. Once we were in the air the stewardess began to pass out drinks, alcohol! I looked around and our guys were accepting the wine, beer, and whiskey hand over fist and stuffing it in their pockets. I went to where Coach Carpenter was sitting and told him what was going on and he said, "Go get it!" I wrangled up a pasteboard box and proceeded to go player to player and separate them from the liquor. Our guys never complained but the A & I guys reported me to their coaches, yelling, "Hey, Coach, he's taking their booze!" The A & I staff did not have an alcohol policy as did we. The whole trip our guys had to hide their drinking from us while the A & I players and coaches drank at the same bars.

Berlin, Germany

We flew directly to Berlin and when we landed we expected a greeting party with directions, porters, and some type of organization; none of that occurred. After deplaning we were faced with a mountain of baggage which was comprised of equipment, uniforms, training supplies, cases of tape and bandages. "Too much sugar for a dime," as Coach Carpenter put it! We were like first-time cruisers; we had packed far too much gear for comfort.

After realizing that we were our own porters we loaded the tour buses that had been provided for our in-country travel and we set out for our lodging. We were dismayed to find that A & I had been quartered in a nice hotel while we were to stay in a youth hostel in a seedy part of Berlin. The sight of our first German meal made the quarters look good and the quarters did not look good! The dining area was laid out with small tables that sat four persons and each table had a soup tureen, four bowls, and a basket of rock-hard rolls. The tureens resembled chamber pots and the thin gruel-like soup within them had four bratwursts floating around that resembled the contents of what might be in a chamber pot! Several of the players's gagged and stumbled away from the tables, revealing the weak stomachs of pampered people. I sat down at a table that had been evacuated and enjoyed the four brats left for the iron gutted. The hard rolls and butter went down well and I carried some to my room for midnight snacks. Needless to say, I was one of the few people on the trip who managed to gain weight.

Coach Carpenter was his usual self, being the head coach and seeing to the needs of his players. Sabra, Coach Carpenter's beautiful wife, was on the trip as was Bradley's wife, Flo. Billy Bock and I were alone and became roommates. Coach Sawyer, our associate athletics director, was also on the trip.

I spoke more German than anyone else in our party so I was given the job of translator. Coach Carpenter would say, "George, tell that SOB to ———," and I would to the best of my ability. Many times my German fell far short of the task and then all hell would ensue. All in all, though, it was a great trip. Aside from the fact that we could not beat A & I, it could not have been much better.

We played the first game of the trip in the famous Olympic stadium in which Jesse Owens was snubbed by Adolf Hitler in 1936. We discussed the history of the place and we were able to see some of the scars of World War Two still on the city of Berlin. It was a great history lesson for the young men and women traveling with us, many of them flying for the first time. We were able to have a catered lunch in downtown Berlin near the still bombed-out Brandenburg church. A lesson in Germanic organization came when it was discovered that the person who set up the meal had inadvertently ordered two meals fewer than what we needed. We called over the manager of the large restaurant and told him we needed two more meals. He haughtily replied that it could not be done; there were no more meals available. Culture shock set in, in America that would have been no problem!

Many of the young men on the trip had never been on an airplane, much less out of the country and they literally got their eyes opened on this trip. When we played our first game in Berlin, the sponsors, who had financed several similar tours with American basketball, told us that we could not huddle and that we should throw passes 50 percent of the time, unheard of in this era of "three yards and a cloud of dust" offenses. There could be no blitzing and we should, generally, keep the game at a fast pace. Both A & I and HSU were basically running teams so we just ignored those bits of advice and went about waging the type of war that got us there.

The Berlin stadium had a golf course-like turf, fine grass with roots about one inch deep. The grounds keepers did not want us to warm up on the field. We milled around a little and then just took the field by stampeding out there and lining up. Coming out of the tunnel to go on to the field an old German was standing in the tunnel's entrance and when one of our black players trotted by he would say, "N——r goot player! N——r goot sportsman!" With his eyes as big as saucers one of our guys said to Coach Carpenter, "Coach, did you hear what he said?" Coach Carpenter with his typical humor, said, "Get on out there, boy. He don't know what the hell he is saying!" We tore up divots all over that fine turfed field but when we came out after the half the field looked just like it did before we went out! The grounds crew, which must have consisted of one hundred men, replaced each divot for the second half.

With this first game we did not know how the crowd would be or even if there would be a crowd. Remember, this was a first. No one knew if Europeans would even be interested in American football. Five minutes before the kickoff time there were maybe twenty people in the stadium besides the two teams and their parties. Considering the fact that this stadium would accommodate 110,000 people, we felt a trifle alone. On the stroke of the announced game time 25,000 people walked in and sat down. It was like time-lapse photography! The crowd went from no people to 25,000 people in what seemed like seconds!

I have few memories of the game but I learned a lesson from Coach Carpenter just before the kickoff. We had the ball and this was to be my first duty as offensive coordinator. I turned to Coach Carpenter and asked, "What you want to run, Coach?" Our eyes met and he said, "George, I'm going to be the offensive line coach and head coach, you are the offensive coordinator, you run what you think is best." That was the way it was to be for the next fifteen years. He was the most courageous, loyal man I ever had the pleasure to work with.

We lost the first game, 17–8, a respectable score but a bitter defeat. We were traveling with them and they were in our face all the time. In my seventeen years with him, Coach Carpenter never brow beat a team or his coaches. This trip was to be no exception, and we pressed on.

After the game we limped back to our hostel and A & I returned to their posh hotel.

Coach Carpenter had tapped me as "discipline coach" upon my arrival and the duty was mine for this trip and throughout my tenure with him. As the discipline coach I was required to tuck in the players on the trip and we established a normal curfew time of eleven o'clock even though we were in Europe. That night after the first game I sat on the stairs in the youth hostel and counted heads as our troops dutifully trekked in from wherever they had gone after the game. Anyone who has ever had the pleasure of keeping football players in line will tell you that once you have squared them away at night you cannot just go on to bed and have any assurance that they will not get up as soon as your door is closed and maybe reestablish some contact they have had to leave before they finished their objectives! This required me to stay up later than they did. I was still sitting on the stairs long after our last player was asleep, which was about one o'clock A.M., when the door to the hostel burst open and in walked two or three of the A & I guys, one being their quarterback, looking for our cheerleaders. Our party boasted fourteen cheerleaders, some of whom were not even students at HSU. We were allowed X number of individuals for our official party. I don't remember how many slots we had and the facts have been lost to history but toward the departure date we began to realize that we were going to have some empty seats if we didn't find more people to sign up for the trip. Can you imagine, free room, board, and travel fare to Europe and not enough takers to fill the bill? Coach Carpenter announced that we would ask around to see if we could get some cheerleaders to go. That sounded great to the players, not so great to the discipline coach. I was apprehensive to say the least. I knew that beer was like water in Europe and that our young men would likely get hold of some on the trip. And now, we would have to deal with females, too?

As it turned out, the young women in our party behaved with impeccable decorum and were no problem on the trip. That night I stood between the randy A & I athletes and the flower of young womanhood in our care. "Where are the cheerleaders?" queried the spokesman for the pack of aroused invaders. "Where you can't get to them." I said, "Turn yourselves around and get on out of here." And they did. That was their last attempt to contact our fair damsels in our quarters at least.

We exited Berlin by bus, going through the famous "Check point Charlie," where the East German guards with submachine guns got on the buses and looked at each passport carefully. It was easy to see that they meant business. None of them cracked a smile and the only squiggle came when a border guard approached my seat on the bus. Billy Bock, my seat mate, pointed to his passport photo and then to mine and said, "Twins." The border guard's expression changed ever so slightly as he scrutinized the two photos with increased intensity. He evidently spoke very good English, but never said a word as he slowly moved past us to the next person. Billy was a practical joker of the highest order and enjoyed my terror from this encounter.

Vienna, Austria

Our second stop on the tour was Austria. Looking back it seems so much like a wonderful dream. We drove on the famous German autobahn, officially named, Bundesautobah, as often as our itinerary would allow. The German autobahn network has a total length of about 12,200 km, or 7,580 miles. At that time the autobahn system was second only to the U.S. Interstate system. The view of the German and Austrian countryside was breathtaking. The Alps were visible much of the trip and the snow-capped peaks were a constant target of our party's various styles of cameras. Our horizons were broadened considerably!

During this first leg of the journey upon which we had to deal with German drivers, Coach Carpenter would look to me to give the drivers their directions. He would say, "George, tell that SOB to stop at the next rest stop, these kids need to water their lilies." That meant we needed to make a pit stop. Or he would say, "Damn it, George, tell him to slow down, he's gonna kill us all!" His concern was totally for the young men and women in our charge. I have never known a more dedicated man.

Our buses crept into Vienna late in the night and, to our surprise, our accommodations were much different from the Berlin youth hostel. We looked up from our bus windows at the majestic Intercontinental Hotel, one of the finest in the city, and could not believe we were going to be quartered there. Texas A & I's buses were in caravan with us and they disembarked like the herd of Javelinas that they were and stormed the hotel. Loud and boisterous, they attracted lots of attention with their noise and considerable size.

Our young men and women were refreshingly different, adhering to Coach Carpenter's admonition to act like you have had some raisin'! They did. The hotel was magnificent. Old European style and cosmopolitan to the core! The influx of energy was noticeable to put it mildly; the little old European men and women sitting in or walking through the lobby were visibly shaken!

Our rooms were large, almost suite like with a fully stocked wine, beer, and liquor refrigerator in each room. As soon as I saw the potable supply I knew we were in trouble. None of our players had ever stayed in such an environment. I literally ran to Coach Carpenter's room and as I did, I saw an empty wine bottle go by one of the windows and crash into the overhang of the hotel entrance. The A & I players had thought the same thing our men were undoubtedly thinking, free liquor! We hit the panic button and dispatched all coaches to our assigned rooms to warn our guys that the bottles emptied would be charged to the offending member's room and that hell would be to pay along with the liquor bill! Throwing the empty bottle out the window would not remove the evidence. We had a couple of imbibers but for the most part few offenders. I believe that the A & I bunch drank every ounce of liquor in their rooms the first night and ran up a considerable tab for the stay.

The sun rose on an excited bunch of Reddies that first morning in Vienna. We were slated for our first practice and also a chance to sightsee some.

We practiced every day that we didn't play with the exception of Sunday. Now, we were slated to play five games in three weeks, a daunting task by any measure. Our practices were Friday practice-like but still taxing because of logistics.

By this time, the mundane task of laundry reared its ugly head. I was able to speak and understand the language, so Coach Carpenter added laundry coach to my list of duties. I didn't mind but I was not exactly schooled in the fine art of laundry. My first venture out into the city of Vienna to find a laundromat resulted in a mini-catastrophe of sorts. We had brand-new red work-out shorts and by this time they no longer smelled like a rose. I asked Coach Carpenter as I exited the hotel lobby if he thought it would be all right to wash everything together. He said it would be fine; it was not. We were fortunate to have had the foresight to bring two colors of game pants on the trip because after the ill-fated laundry junket all our gray game pants were a bright pink! We wore our red pants for the remainder of the trip and, to his credit, Coach Carpenter never mentioned my ignorance in the laundry area.

After our first practice we literally turned our charges loose in the cultured city of Vienna and they scattered like the proverbial covey of quail! I could tell Coach Carpenter was nervous about the relinquishing of control but he wanted them to get the maximum benefit of the trip and you must let them have wings, as the saying goes. We did.

The guys came back to the hotel for meals and they were chattering to one another and we heard about the wonderful trolley system they had been using all day. Almost all of them thought it was free because they operated under the honor system. You bought tokens and used them according to the instructions on each trolley. Our men were used to bus drivers taking tickets and these trolley operators did not do that, so, it was free! There were random checks and it was considered a serious offense to steal a ride. We straightened this out and all was fine.

We practiced and played in Prater Stadium, Austria's national stadium. Prater Stadium is in Prater Park, a conglomerate of mind-dazzling mechanisms and marvels designed to entertain and fascinate. The famous Lipizzaner Stallions are housed and trained in Prater Park and the world famous giant Riesenrad Ferris wheel has been there since 1897. High cotton for an old boy from Hamburg, Arkansas!

We lost the second game, 21–7 this time. We knew full well that these losses would be covered by historical dust; we still suffered each one as a loss! "That is why they keep score, buddy ruff!" Coach was prone to say. First is first and second is nothing! We endured.

In Vienna we were approached by an independent journalist, an American, born in Vienna, taken to America by his soldier father and Austrian mother and reared in our country. He had served in Vietnam honorably but had become disenchanted by our culture and had relinquished his American citizenship and returned to Austria to raise his family. He asked for permission to film our practices and our game for a documentary. Initially, Coach Carpenter agreed but after learning that the guy had left our country for good Coach asked the man to leave us alone. When the guy asked why, Coach said, "You left the greatest country in the world, get out of my sight!" R. L. Carpenter was a patriot!

Nuremburg, Germany

Our next stop was to be Nuremburg, back in Germany. I was excited about the proximity of Nuremburg to Dachau, one of Adolph Hitler's notorious work camps of World War Two. My father had been one of the first soldiers of the storied Forty-fifth Division, the Thunderbirds, to enter the compound in 1945. I hoped we would get to visit the site. Coach Carpenter learned of my connection to Dachau so he arranged for a tour of the sinister reminder of a nation gone mad. I was very grateful.

We arrived in the historic city of Nuremburg in the late afternoon and were quartered this time in a swank old hotel near downtown Nuremburg, in walking distance from Main Street. By this time our troops were becoming hungry for some good old American food. There was an American military facility nearby so the promoters of the trip arranged for our party to eat on the base one day. We pigged out, demonstrating to the army cooks that we enjoyed their food.

One of the first people we encountered on the base was Tex Curtner, a guy Coach Carpenter taught at Wynne High School ten or so years before. Tex was very glad to see his old coach and teacher. Tex had been one of Coach's student managers at Wynne, and Tex was very helpful to us for the remainder of our stay in Nuremburg. The term "small world" comes to mind here. Tex was unaware that we were in Germany and, of course, Coach Carpenter had no idea Tex was around.

Coach Carpenter was all about taking care of the troops. He was vigilant and careful to see that each young man was comfortable and that he had everything he needed. The coaches on the trip, myself, Bradley Mills, Billy Bock, and our graduate assistant, Mike Deal, along with our volunteer trainer, Brother Bob Trieschmann, were all anxious to be about sightseeing in this treasure trove of German history. Coach Carpenter exercised his force of will to bend us to his plans. He was a master of thoughtful suggestion and a very astute psychologist. His skill and the wonderful leadership abilities of our associate athletics director, Jim Mack Sawyer, made the trip smooth and a joy to all aboard.

One way to judge the level of a person's skill in a particular endeavor is by the ease in which they accomplish a specific task. Coach Carpenter captained this trip and from the outside it looked so easy. It was not. We lost the game played in Nuremburg, also, 17 to 15. We played the game on Adolph Hitler's Zeppelin Field, which had an interior area larger than that of twelve football fields and would seat up to two hundred thousand people! Estimates said that there were probably twenty-five thousand people there, many of them GIs from the large army base.

Probably my sharpest memory of the field and the stop in Nuremburg centered on our walk-through the day before we played the game when our players saw some German laborers take a break from digging a trench for plumbing and opening up their lunch boxes and popping the tab on a couple of beers! That impressed most of them. The historic field was kind of an afterthought to them, no big deal.

Throughout the trip we were able to take tours of the area in which we were staying. Nuremburg was kind of a highlight in a way because of the rich history there.

Our stop in Nuremburg was the longest on the excursion. The reason for this fact is that after playing the game we packed our considerable gear and got on the buses and headed out for Rome, Italy. Before exiting the Nuremburg city limits we were stopped by German police with flashing lights and honking horns. At first I thought we might have been guilty of not paying our hotel bill. Instead, the authorities in Italy had decided that we might be too tempting a target for political protesters since it was election time in Italy. At that time, before the fall of the Berlin wall and the collapse of Communism, the political unrest was caused, for the most part, by the Communists. We had to go to plan B.

Changing plans for almost two hundred people is difficult in the good old USA, it is infinitely more so in Europe. The promoters had to find a field that would do for our brand of football. Remember that this was a first. Food and rooms for the parties and travel arrangements amounted to a gargantuan task! The promoters came through. While we waited on the buses for a couple of hours, the administration and logistic crew went to work and we were on board for that plan B. We checked back into the same hotel, same rooms, etc., and learned that we would play our next game in Mannheim, Germany, on another large army base.

Manheim, Germany

We traveled by railway to Manheim and this was another experience of a lifetime! Railway travel in Europe is eons ahead of the railway system in the United States. From the lack of rail clatter to the sleeping cars to the virtual ease of operation of the complete system, it is a pleasure to use. Imagine that you are a German or any European citizen on a train that is invaded by a large group of active young men who naturally exude a physical prescience and tend to stand out in any setting. I think we caused more than a little emotional discomfort even though we were not overly loud.

The trip to and from Manheim was smooth as a baby's butt, as Coach Carpenter would say, except for the game. We lost. Twenty to six was the largest margin of defeat suffered by the Reddie team on the tour. We endured. Each loss increased our resolve to win but the Javelinas were tougher than a cheap steak. Their quarterback was a master of the veer offense and even our great defense and the architect of that defense, Bradley Mills, could not hold them long. We had now lost four of four to the gridironers from Kingsville, four bitter pills crammed down our collective throats with considerable vigor!

After the game in Manheim and the return trip to Nuremburg, we packed our grips and boarded the buses for Paris, France. "How you going to keep them down on the farm once they have seen Paree" fits so well! By this time our players were almost cosmopolitan. They had seen the elephant. With four games under their belts the youngest squad members had almost a half a season's experience. That half season was against the best competition in the nation no less. We were getting better but unfortunately, so were the Javelinas!

Paris, France

We took Paris by storm, well, maybe by a little less wind, perhaps by a gust. At any rate, we were on location at the point most all of us had targeted as the main event. Paris, France, we had a new language to master, a new culture to explore. Our players, as soon as we set foot down in Paris, began to speak their Arkansasese with a French accent! When will zee meel be served? Where is my bed droom? Some actually thought they were fluent in French.

Our coaching staff, Coach Carpenter included, was more relaxed on this last leg of our journey than we had been the entire trip. For the first time, we did not practice every day. We hit the City of Lights like a linebacker blitz! We sightsaw our butts off as Coach Carpenter put it. The Louvre, Notre Dame Cathedral, the Eiffel Tower, the Musee d'Orsay, the Arc de Triomphe, and the Champs-Elysees and, of course, Sacre Coeur and Montmartre. We saw them all and more. We roamed the streets of Paris in a frenzy born of the knowledge that our time in Europe was short.

A couple of memorable experiences spring to mind here; one concerned our volunteer trainer and team chaplin, Brother Bob Tieishmann. Brother Bob was a large man in more ways than size. He had a large voice, a large appetite, and a large heart. He was all wool and a yard wide as described by Coach Carpenter. On our first day of seeing Paris we mounted the Eiffel Tower during peak hours and were bombarded by constant announcements of "beware of pickpockets!" Coach Carpenter allowed as to how "they are thicker than fleas on a dog's back!" I eased up to Brother Bob and grabbed hold of his wallet. He whirled around and grabbed my hand in his ham-like paw and announced to no one in particular, "I've got it!" A few hours later, while a group of us were crowding on to the Paris Metro, Brother Bob, seeing that some of the bunch might not be able to get on the overflowing car, backed off and ran through the door using his considerable bulk to smash and compact the passengers to make room. Already on board I felt an arm brush my lower legs and about that time I heard Brother Bob yell, "My wallet!" The crafty pickpockets residing in the Montmartre district had succeeded where the Eiffel pirates had failed. The train door closed and off we went. Brother Bob, feeling his wallet being lifted, whirled around and bear hugged the culprit but the thief had thrown the wallet on the floor of the car and his colleague standing outside the conveyance simply reached in and snagged the billfold as the door closed and the train sped off! Slick as a whistle! We had to spend most of the next day in a French police station reporting the theft. I might add here that as we entered the police station that morning, Coach Carpenter looked around and, to my horror, spit a large chew of Red Man tobacco behind the front door. Fortunately for us, none of the gendarmes saw this happen. The policemen in the station were very curious about us and amused by our Arkansas drawls. They were very nice and even participated in an attempted practical joke instigated by Billy Bock, who got them to pretend to arrest me. I had seen the movie *Papillion* only a couple of years before this and the idea of a French jail conjured up some frightening images.

Game day rushed upon us; as the saying goes, time flies when you are having fun. Not a soul on the trip failed to have fun in Paris! When we questioned the tour logistical crew about travel to the game they replied that we would ride the Metro to the game. The hell we will replied Coach Carpenter, get us some buses or the game is off. Again, the crew scrambled around and found enough buses to do the job. I still marvel today considering the pace at which the European culture operates. Late in the day, in Paris France they found four buses to transport the party. The driver on our bus was surly and did not want to wait for some stragglers from our team. He started the bus and prepared to leave some of our guys. "Stop him, George!" Coach yelled. So I reached over and switched the bus off and threw the keys out the door. To my chagrin, the bus continued to run but the driver had to get out to retrieve the keys. By this time the young men in question showed up, and we sped away for the Stade Saint-Germain, the site of our last game. We had a large crowd, estimated to be 25,000 plus with about that many watching from nearby high rises. We got lots of publicity, there was much interest. I remember that the French had no words to describe American football positions, for instance, they called linebackers, la braziers, translated, stoppers! There were French movie stars taking photo ops and American and French military brass out in abundance. We played our hearts out and lost, 21–13. O for five!

The remainder of the trip went like the first, quick and smooth. Our young men did not miss a lick. We had no incident in which any member of our group was involved in any mishap, no punishment was necessary and none was meted out. The conduct of our young men is a high compliment to the staff of our football team, Coach R. L. Sporty Carpenter, Coach Bradley Mills, Coach Billy Bock, graduate assistant Mike Deal, Brother Bob Trieschmann, and our associate athletics director Coach Jim Mack Sawyer, all of whom have passed away with the exception of Mike. We practiced careful and constant supervision throughout the trip but the cooperation of our group indicates that they knew full well that they were doing something larger than themselves and that that they represented the United States as well as the Reddie Nation. They were determined to refute the "ugly American" image and they did so in a convincing manner.

Next stop, Arkadelphia!

REDDIE FOOTBALL HALL OF FAME

Legends

When one coaches a young man or young woman or a boy or girl, a bond may ensue. Hopefully this is a bond of friendship, loyalty, and love. The ability to forge such a bond is not presumed when one obtains the title of coach. R. L. Carpenter could and did forge such bonds. He did not practice the art of friendship to further his cause but the capacity to endear was an integral element of his persona. In our times together we often spoke of individuals who were "legends in their own minds." Paper tigers, blow hards, zeros, and other descriptors to indicate a distrust of some kind. These discussions were private and not privy to outside ears. When we discussed our players or individuals attempting to become players, the feeling changed. R. L. Carpenter was a man of unusual patronage. He loved deeply and clung to his charges fiercely! Often, while discussing our troupes he would be overcome with emotion and have to clear his throat before going on. If the individual had graduated or had parted in any manner he was even more likely to have the misty-eyed state arise. I grew to expect it and, indeed, it was more than a little contagious. Now, we didn't sit around crying. But his demeanor encouraged in me the feeling for people in general. He often exhorted his coaches to treat our charges as if they were our sons, a practice that I feel should be mandatory in all sports today!

What I am saying is that to R. L. Carpenter every one of his players was to him a legend. A list would contain, without regard to size or ability or year of graduation, the following names, and I pray that I have not missed anyone: Calvin Johnson (deceased), Steve King (deceased), Danny Howard (deceased), Tony Height (deceased), Arvester "Kool Aid" Brown (deceased), Roscoe White (deceased),

James "Dish" Dishroom (deceased), Mike Griffith (deceased), James Morehart (deceased), Brian Prunty (deceased), Charles "Smokey" Cummings (deceased), Danny Abernathy, Bayon Abraham, Bo Adkisson, Kip Agee, Ricky Agee, Jack "Three Fingered Jack" Alvarez, David "Air Fern" Amerson, Clarence Ray Arnold, Richie "Boomer" Arthur, Mike Atkins, Jeff Atkinson, Dan Backus, Bruce Bailey, Bryan Bailey, Darwin Bailey, Paul Bailey, Robert Bailey, Randy Ballard, Bruce Barnes, Chester Barnes, Mike Bass, Terry Bell, Tony Beltrani, Don Benton, Ron Benton, Jasper Benton, Ira Benton, Rueben Benton, John Beverburg, Glen Biddle, Phillip Billings, Lenny Bishop, Terry Blaylock, Sam Blocker, Ricky Borkins, Doug Botwell, Herman Botley, Bob Boullion, Charley Boyd, Don Braddock, Ron Braddock, Rodney Bragg, Ron Brazell, John Briggs, Ron Briggs, Donnell Brooks, Sonny Brooks, Terrance Anthony "TAB" Brown, Eric Brown, Wendell Bruno, Keith Bryan, Marvell Burgess, Ronnie Burnett, Roy Burton, Jim Bush, James Butler, Danny Byars, Jeffery Calaham, Terry "Pump" Calkins, Samuel Calvin, Pat Campbell, Vernon Campbell, Dick Carmichael, David Carpenter, Sam Carr, Jim Carter, Jodi Carter, Donald Castleberry, Leonard Cates, John Charbonneau, Anthony Cheeks, Willy Christianson, Rex Chronister, Richard Clark, Joe Coffield, Steve Colbert, Bobby Cole, Andy Coleman, Don Cooley, Robert Cooley, Dewayne "Corny" Cornelious, John Cornelious, Andre Crawford, Victor Crews, David Crommet, Alan Crook, Charles Crook, Jerry Cunningham, Todd Curtis, Lee Daily, Elbert Daniels, Alvin Darden, Ronald Davidson, John Davie, Brian Davis, Jerry Mack Davis, John Davis, Mark "Mad Dog" Davis, Eric Dawson, Larry Day, Leonard Delagarza, Mark Delany, Bruce Dickerson, Jimmy Dill, James Dixon, Phillip Dobbins, Charley Doles, Duke Drews, Mike Duke, Terry Duncan, Terry Eason, Phillip Echols, Tyrone Echols, Carlos Edmonson, Randy Elliot, Tom Elliot, Jerran Etherly, Tony Evans, Herbert Farr, Craig Fant, Richard Faulkner, Kenny Fells, Joe Flemmons, Ricky Flenory, Mike Flournoy,

Jim Ford, John Ford, John "Big John" Ford, Danny Foreman, Daryl "Poof" Foreman, Don Forrester, Tracy Forte, Tyrone Forte, Byron Foster, Eddie Fullwood, Ben Fulton, Larry Gartman, Tony Gant, Terry Gibbs, Nathan Gills, Ricky Glidewell, William Gober, Robert Godbolt, Bob Goldhorn, Jim Goode, Calvin Goshen, Maurice Grant, Ralph Graves, Joey Green, Theodore Green, Virgil Green, Roy Green, Robert Greenup, Dorsey Griffin, J. B. Grimes, Mark Grimes, Johnny Gross, Jaron Guess, Lee Hammond, Ron Hampton, John Hanie, John Harding, Al Harrell, Don Harrison, Dan Harshfield, Tommy Hart, Jeff Haskins, Kenny Haskins, Danilo Haynes, Sylvester Henry, Charles Hesser, Robert Hester, Chris Hicken, Daryl Hightower, Leon Hodge, Tom Hogan, Jay Holland, Jakie Honea, Randy Hornbeck, Richard Houston, Brian Howard, Steve Hughes, Micah Hullet, David Humphrey, Daniel Hunter, James Hunter, Wilbert Hunter, Charles Jackson, Gary Jackson, Jeff Jackson, Jerry Jackson, Leroy Jackson, Greg Jacobs, Horace Jennings, Tony Johns, Dennis Johnson, James Johnson, Jimmy Johnson, L. B. Johnson, Mike Johnson, Ronnie Johnson, Silas Johnson, Wayne Johnson, Kaward Jolly, Bobby Jones, Byron Jones, Cory Jones, Curtis Jones, Rodney Jones, Sparta Jordan, Victor Jordan, David Kee, Terry Kelly, Robert Kilby, Milton Kimble, Joel Kirkpatrick, John Kitchens, Darrell Krimminger, Ken Kruitchof, Jeff Kubacak, George Lafargue, Ricky Laird, Jason Leavitt, Billy Lefear, Cantrell Lewis, Dexter Lewis, Gary Lewis, Nat Lewis, Ronnie Lewis, Tony Lewis, John Lindgren, Danny Lindsey, Larry Locke, Pat Longinotti, Walt Lowe, Mike Mack, Gus Malzahn, Ken Mann, Mickey Mapes, David Martin, Harry Massey, Larry McAllister, Bud McBride, James McBride, Jeff McCann, Gary McCauley, Melvin McCline, Jesse "Bubba" McCray, D. C. McDonald, Greg McGhee, Ricky McGill, Pat McGuire, Steve McGuire, Marc Menefee, Howard Mills, Joe Mills, Rickey Minter, Bernard Mitchell, Steve Mitchell, Barry Mobley, Butch Monticello, David Moore, Greg Moore, Larry Morehart, Jim Morgan, Randy

Morgan, Jim Morris, Charley Moseley, Andre Muldrew, Trent Nalepa, Roland Nash, Mike Nazarenko, Kevin Nelson, Milton Nelson, Kris Nichols, Jim Norman, Glen Norris, Rickey Norris, Andy O'Mara, Darren O. Quinn, Ralph Ohm, Roy Optiz, Dave Osborn, Columbus Osby, Gary Overturff, Jerome Pace, Stan Pace, Don Paladino, Drew Parker, Stan Parris, Mike Parker, Ned Parrette, Mike Pasley, John Patterson, Phil Patterson, Donald Patton, Ronald Patton, Ricky Patton, Tyrone Paysinger, Frank "Flash" Pearson, Arthur Periot, Rick Pennington, Larry Perrin, Doug Pilcher, Mark Pilcher, Joe Pitts, George Pledger, Kyle Preston, Lewis Pryor, Terry Quast, Mackey Ramsey, Allen Ray, Larry "Baby" Ray, Dennis Ray, Mike Reynolds, Ray Reynolds, Earnest Rhone, John Rhone, Jimmy Rice, Elgie Richards, Ricky Richards, Ryan Richardson, Stan Riner, Harold Ringgold, Tony Roberts, Billy Robinson, Eric Robinson, Paul Robinson, Danny Rogers, Terry Rogers, Gary Rollins, Craig Romine, Rusty Ross, Brian Rowley, Bob Samuels, Mark Sanders, Lester Scroggins, Gary Segrest, Tony Sergio, Tim Shavers, Chris Shead, Lance Sisk, Benny Skaggs, Andrew Smith, Joe Smith, Larry Smith, Phillip Smith, Troy Smith, Willie Smith, John Smithers, Donald Solco, Lloyd Speck, Reggie Speights, David Starks, Greg Stewart, Tommy Stiffler, Earnest Stokes, Gene Stubber, Mike Tedford, Lawrence Texada, Don Thomas, Blake Thompson, Larry "Monk" Thompson, Randy Thompson, Ronnie Thornton, Thresher Howard, Don Tison, Tyce Tobola, Roy Tomlinson, John Truit, James Tubbs, Mike Vaughn, Rickey Vinson, Mark Voss, Mike Wade, Walter Waits, Charles Walker, Gus Walker, Kenny Walker, Dean Wall, James Walton, Alan Ward, Talmadge Ward, Bruce Watters, Clarence Watkins, Claude Watkins, Russel Weatherly, Jim West, Duane White, James White, Randy White, Terrance White, David Whitener, Daryl "Peabo" Wilkins, Drew Wilkins, Troy Wilkins, Fred Williams, Greg "Skip" Williams, Donnie Willis, Ray Willis, Steve Winston, Duke Womack, Roland Womack, Matt Woodruff, Jerry Wright, Morris "Tank"

Wright, Joe Yancy, Robert Yancey, Jim "Yard Dog" Yarberry, Ivory Young, Lynn Young, Ronny Young, Scott Young.

These young men were the delight of his life.

CHAPTER FOUR

All Good Things . . .

The European excursion shortened the Reddie staff's summer considerably and we were behind in recruiting. Coach Carpenter hit the ground running as soon as the plane touched the runway in Little Rock. He was known to be a fierce recruiter and it did not set well with him that he had lost so much valuable time in this most important part of college football.

It was our practice to recruit not only for players but also for young men who might stick on campus in the event that they did not make the squad. This increased the degree of difficulty by a lot but it is how Coach Carpenter helped nurture his alma mater. His concern for the complete university resulted in many young men being motivated to go to college and graduate when their ability to play football was highly suspect. The happy side of this happenstance is that numerous times the talent suspect player would mature and become a scorpion as we called great players. A long list of these transformers comes to mind, too long to list each, so I will single out one who became our icon for big desire and small of stature and gridiron gifts. Jasper Benton came to us from tiny Norphlet, Arkansas, near Eldorado. Jasper reported to our camp as a linebacker but looked more like a small wide receiver. During fall two-a-day practices Jasper Benton drew minuscule notice from his position coach. He was not a zero, a label for nonhitters. He would hit you with everything he had, which we have already established was not much! In terms used in academia, he was an overachiever. In college football an overachiever linebacker is fine if he is 6'4 and 240 lbs. and runs the 40-yard dash in 4.5 seconds! Short of that kind of standard causes one to recruit for the non-eyeball reject. Jasper will not mind me calling him an eyeball reject, because he was. At the end of fall practice, when scholarships were announced, Coach Carpenter called in all of the squad and had a private, one-on-one meeting with each one of them. That particular year we had so many prospects on the squad we had to borrow helmets from Arkadelphia High School.

Now, Coach Carpenter never relished cutting a player but the number situation forced him to this extreme measure. When Jasper came into the head coach's office he received the same treatment as Terry Blaylock, Joe Smith, or Larry McAlister, all stars on the team. Coach Carpenter was a master at relating to players and people in general. After some small talk the dreaded axe fell, "Son, you need to concentrate on your studies, lift weights, get bigger, and come back out in the spring." Our staff had discussed at length each player and a consensus was that Jasper was not large enough to help us win and in all probability, he would never be. What we had failed to notice in the short fall session rife with great talent was that Jasper Benton had the eye of the tiger! It is always difficult to judge the size of the fight in the dog until one has had the dog in the fight! Jasper's eyes welled up with tears, revealing his substantial pride. "Coach," he said, "please don't cut me. I love football, I must play!" That was all it took for Coach Carpenter to make an executive decision and allow Jasper Benton to remain on the squad. The heart-swelling, chest-thumping end of the Jasper Benton story is that he grew some, he worked incredibly hard, and before the season was over he drew attention from all the coaches, most of whom were themselves overachievers. Jasper Benton would knock your liver out! Jasper Benton had no regard for his personal safety. Jasper Benton would get right in your mustache! Jasper Benton was a player! Jasper Benton returned three passes for touchdowns his junior year and was a team leader all four years as a Reddie. I feel comfortable in saying that Coach Carpenter was most proud of Jasper when he graduated from college and was commissioned in the United States Army as a second lieutenant. As a result of Jasper sticking at Henderson State, his two younger brothers, Ira and Rueben, came and played for us. They are stories in themselves and were of the same caliber as Jasper, fine men and good productive citizens now. A huge return on a gesture of faith in a small dog!

There were other inspiring young men in the years I spent coaching with Coach Carpenter, many in fact. If the hallowed ground of Carpenter-Haygood Stadium could speak, it would shout the names of men like Joe Smith, Louis Pryor, Curtis Jones, Roy Green, Johnny Gross, Lynn Young, Calvin Johnson, Larry Locke, Joe Yancy, Lawrence Texada, and many others who strove for victory on its grassy span. The stadium and Henderson State would be equally proud of the men like Bobby Cole, Arvester Brown, Theodore Green, Wayne Davenport, Dan Cathy, Carl Humphrey, and scores of others who worked as hard as anyone else but served to stand and wait or labor as managers.

There are far too many to mention in this space but there will be a "Sporty Honor roll" at the close of this book.

We took two sophomore quarterbacks to Europe and we naturally thought one of them would start and the other would be an experienced back up. Terry Blaylock had finished his brilliant career and had been the starter so long no one else had much experience save the two guys mentioned before. The last three years of Blaylock's career the Reddies were 32 and 4, one of those losses being in the finals of the NAIA National Championship game in Kingsville, Texas. We knew Terry was going to be like the man in the circus who was shot out of the cannon; it would be hard to replace a man of his caliber!

Sure enough, we started the 1976 season out fairly strong, beating Central Oklahoma 9–0 and Arkansas Tech 28–0. The very next week we stumbled against conference opponent Harding, losing

20–15. We had stuck to our plan to use the two young men we had with us on the trip but they were not pleasing us with their play. It was a matter of ability and not their fault. We recruited them, we coached them, and we took the blame. But, a bright star had stepped off the bus that fall and he came into the Harding game after it was apparent we were about to lose it. I think we were down 20–0 when George Sparks went into the game. One of the guys in the huddle said George sprinted out to the huddle and said, "Hell, men, we've got to do something," and they did. When the whistle blew we were clawing our way back to the tune of 15–20 and a new era had begun! George Sparks could play; he had game as the later generations say. He was probably as good when he arrived in camp as he was to be, but he could do it all. George could run and throw and he was smart to boot. George came to us from Port Arthur High School in Port Arthur, Texas, sent by Greg Green from Sparkman, Arkansas. Greg was dubbed for eternity as "goose" by Coach Carpenter and he wears the name with pride, a fine Reddie alumni! Greg was instrumental in Port Arthur hiring Joe Smith to his first and only coaching job. Joe has worked in the Port Arthur System for over thirty-two years now. Joe, Greg, and friends of Coach Carpenter in that football-rich part of the country have sent numerous athletes to Henderson State over the past thirty-eight years. A stream of talented, well-coached young men who reflected great pride on their school. The short list includes Lawrence Texada, Darryl "Poof" Foreman, and Donald Solco. Texada was drafted in the eighth round of the NFL draft of 1982. Texada lined up at slot back his freshman year, and I just happened to be near him after his first snap against what was one of the best defenses in the nation, coached by Bradley Mills. Bradley had his defensive backs line up on your outside shoulder and when the ball was snapped they attacked you like a serial killer! Lawrence had never experienced the visceral violence of college football. He staggered back to the huddle, bent over, and grabbed his helmet with both hands and whispered, "My God!" Countless numbers of what we called "want-to- be's" never recovered from this nightmare. They usually quietly packed their bags soon after the awakening and crept away from campus in the still of the night leaving their empty beds to announce their parting. Lawrence was no want-to-be. I watched him the next play and he came off the line with an explosive movement that caused the defensive back to recoil and Lawrence zipped by him and ran a decent pass route. We had a player!

We lost only one more game that year, posting an 8–2 record but that loss was to UCA in our conference and it knocked us out of the championship for that year.

Coach Carpenter's overall record as coach of the Reddie football team was 119–76–5. His winning percentage was .608. His number of victories is far and away larger than any other Reddie coach. His tenure of nineteen years, one more than the legendary Coach Duke Wells, will probably remain forever the longest in Reddie history. The impact he had on the lives of the young men and women who came under his tutelage is incalculable. Coach Duke Wells was his mentor and I think he was much like Coach Wells, a great man who reveled in helping people of all walks of life. They both were known to put their players' welfare above their personal welfare. The interest of their players and their players' families had a tall priority in their scheme of things. Coach Wells and Coach Carpenter had different ways of doing things but they were cut from the same cloth when it came to personal relations. I was fortunate enough to have worked under both of them.

I walked the sidelines and endured the scorching Arkansas heat and the bone-chilling winters with Coach Carpenter for sixteen seasons. We literally traveled the world doing what we both loved, coaching football. He was one of a kind and the stories chronicled within these pages verify that fact. Never a day goes by that I don't think of him in some way, usually it is when I hear a good joke or I hear someone repeat one of his many sayings. I often think I would like to tell Coach about that. We laughed long and hard most every day. We worked long hours while our families grew up dutifully raised by their mamas.

I would be amiss if I didn't mention his intense love for his family and the incredibly private man that he was. He never failed to see to it that I had the opportunity to attend an event in which my children were participating if it was at all possible. He sacrificed time with his own family to give his assistants time with theirs, a huge forfeit. He was loyal to a fault and had the courage to do what he thought was right.

Coach Carpenter was inducted into the Arkansas Sports Hall of Fame in 2002. Here is the information listed there:

> Ralph (Sporty) Carpenter—One of the most successful football coaches in the AIC, paced the sideline at Henderson State University for 19 seasons. He is the winningest coach in HSU history. He had an overall record of 119–76–5. In the early 1970's Henderson won three consecutive AIC championships (1973, 1974 and 1975). In his 19 seasons in the league he had 13 teams to finish in the top 20 in the NAIA poll. After his 5th AIC title in 1985 Sporty was named NAIA Coach of the Year. He served as President of the NAIA Coaches Association. The football stadium at HSU bears his name, "Carpenter-Haygood Stadium." His teams won 5 AIC championships. He had stops as a high school coach at Wynne and Magnolia. He was a native of Monticello.

And so, I come to the end of this labor of love that has taken me far too long to finish. The blame for the lack of a timely finish goes to me. I had to stop at times to laugh at some dusty memory or to pause to wipe a tear of remembrance from my misty eyes. It was a good ride, a hearty journey. We were young, he forty-four or forty-five and I was thirty-two when I joined him. We talked of many subjects and solved many of the world's problems in our minds. We coached hard, we played hard. Once, he and I and Billy Bock and Bradley Mills drove from Arkadelphia to San Francisco and back and never mentioned football a single time! If that isn't a record, it's a damn good average as he would say! We spent so many hours in meetings Coach Carpenter would not subject us to business while on a pleasure trip, one more trait I found to be endearing.

My journey with R. L. "Sporty" Carpenter began in July of 1974 and ended with his death in February of 1990. What a trip. Quad, scripsi, scripsi.